Boston Baby: *A Field Guide for Urban Parents*

Boston Baby: *A Field Guide for Urban Parents*

The ABCs of Navigating the City from Playgrounds to Preschool

Kim Foley MacKinnon

Union Park Press • Boston

Union Park Press
Boston, MA 02118
www.unionparkpress.com

Printed in the United States of America
First Edition

Library of Congress Control
Number: 2009933788
ISBN: 978-1934598-02-3; 1-934598-02-X

Book and cover design by Elizabeth Lawrence.
Book and cover illustrations by Karen Klassen.

Is your business, organization or institution
interested in being listed in the next edition?
Email us at BB@unionparkpress.com.

Contents

While by no means the most affordable city in the country, Boston may be one of the best cities in which to raise a family. Think about it. Boston is a world-class city with fantastic cultural resources, decent public transportation, a rich history, interesting architecture, and wonderful restaurants. It's cosmopolitan and down-to-earth, by turns chic and old-fashioned. The city's location gives residents access to the mountains and seaside, and it is one of the most highly educated metropolitan areas in the nation. That you don't have to reside within the city limits to take advantage of all Boston has to offer is another advantage—whether you live in the suburbs or the city, Boston is as easy to visit as it is to love.

For the past decade, I've been writing about parenting and family activities in and around Boston as a journalist and author. *Boston Baby* takes this information in a different direction. This isn't a book for tourists—there are plenty of those already. Nor is this a book for new parents looking for advice on how to raise their own little Einstein. This is a "survival" guide, a comprehensive resource for families looking to take the rich offerings of their city and incorporate them into their day-to-day lives. The information in this book comes from my own experiences as a journalist covering the family beat, as well as a mother who certainly would've liked to have had this book when my daughter was born. In it, you'll discover everything *Boston Baby*, from where you and your newborn can take classes to restaurants that will welcome your toddler to sites for rainy day play, tips on finding bargains, and day trips for when you must get out of town. Additionally, I've devoted chapters to preschools and the Boston Public School system—believe me when I tell you it is never too early to start thinking about school! Throughout, I've turned to local experts, such as sleep expert Dr. Richard Ferber, *Boston Parents Paper* editor Deirdre Wilson, Isis Maternity founder Johanna McChesney, and *The Boston Globe* columnist Robin Abrahams (aka Miss Conduct), to weigh in with their advice and thoughts.

As you already know, parenthood is an adventure unto itself. The good news is that raising your children in a city as stimulating as Boston will only add to that excitement. Use this handy field guide to make the most of these delightful early years of family life. Throw it in the diaper bag, head out the door, and go have some fun!

Using Your Field Guide

For the purposes of this book, I've included age recommendations when appropriate. Of course, you know your child best—one child might be ready for art lessons at two years old, while another two-year-old might be more interested in eating glue. Generally, ages are defined as follows:

A All ages: Birth on up
I Infants: Birth to one year
T Toddlers: One year to two years, nine months (occasionally written as 2.9)
P Preschoolers: Two years, nine months and up

Keep in mind that age won't always determine which classes are the right fit for you and your child. Some classes, such as mommy and me yoga, are usually only for babies who are not yet crawling. Other classes are best for babies who can sit up and participate, usually around six months.

Everyone knows Boston is a city of neighborhoods—but it's also a city of suburban communities. Geographically, I've limited listings in this book to Boston, Cambridge, Brookline, and Newton—though there are certainly a wealth of treasures to be had in other communities as well, and I've included some when they were simply too good to pass up. The great news is that whether your family lives in Boston or its suburbs, all of the listings and activities included in the field guide are easily reached and worth a little car time.

1 You & Me, Babe

NOTHING COMPARES TO that first flush of parenthood. Those early months are filled with joy, anxiety, surprises, and exhaustion. Getting out of the house can be so daunting that it seems like you're trying to stage a prison break. Believe it or not, you'll eventually be ready to experience this new world with your baby. So, where do you begin?

Here's the best advice I received: find other parents in the same boat. Navigating the life-altering weeks of early parenthood can be lonely work—take it from me. I was the first in my circle of friends to have a child, and when my husband went back to work after a few weeks of paternity leave, I was left to long periods of time each day (eight hours or more!) with just me and my new bundle of joy. While everyone I knew was working or going to graduate school, I was learning the ins and outs of being a mom.

I signed up for a new mom's program at WarmLines, and despite the fact that my daughter hated her car seat and screamed all the way to every meeting, it became my lifeline. Ten years have passed, but I am pleased to say that I'm still friends with two women from that group. We have been there for each other through all the ups and downs of those rocky and exhilarating early years.

Boston and its surrounding communities have an incredible array of activities for newly inducted parents. These programs and groups are parent-centered and aim to support, educate, and connect new parents with each other. Most sessions are run by a facilitator who helps break the ice. If you don't see anything below that appeals to you, don't worry. Boston-area hospitals and birth centers also offer postpartum services (although some hospitals only offer these services to their own patients). If you have a home birth, check with your midwife. The only rule is to pick *something* and get out of the house. Joining a group or class may end up being one of the smartest things you can do for yourself (and your sanity)!

No matter how overjoyed you are about the birth of your child, the first year isn't always a bed of roses. You may need a night nurse, you may have trouble breastfeeding, you may experience a bout of the Baby Blues or find yourself struggling with postpartum depression. Don't be afraid to reach out. At the end of this chapter, you'll find a number of parenting resources to get you through those difficult moments. As you'll see, there are plenty of people who can help. Remember: happy, healthy parents (who are treated to a little sleep now and then) make for happy, healthy babies!

New Parents Support Groups & Classes

Boston Association for Childbirth Education (BACE)/ Nursing Mothers' Council (NMC)
617-244-5102 | www.bace-nmc.org

I Provides childbirth and breastfeeding education and offers a comprehensive, hands-on childbirth instructor certification program along with advanced childbirth training workshops. Visit the website for a list of referred instructors and locations.

Family Nurturing Center of Massachusetts (FNC)
200 Bowdoin Street, Dorchester
617-474-1143 | www.familynurturing.org
Free.

A The FNC is a community-based non-profit that was founded in 1994 to promote healthy families and communities and reduce child maltreatment and abuse. To that end, they offer a variety of neighborhood programs and oversee a number of organizations, including the Allston-Brighton Family Network (ABFN) for Allston-Brighton families with newborns through four years; Stony Brook CARES (serving Roslindale); and Dorchester CARES.

Among others, programs include Nurturing Our Babies, Nurturing for Parents and Children, Teen Parent Nurturing, Nurturing Fathers, and Nurturing for Birth and Foster Families. These programs are all a series of classes for families to take together, usually held at a community meeting place with eight to ten other families. In most cases, there are fifteen weekly sessions, each lasting three hours, run by trained nurturing teams. You'll spend time learning and sharing strategies to increase communication skills, develop family rules, use nurturing discipline, address conflict, share feelings, and enjoy family fun.

Isis Maternity

Arlington: 397 Massachusetts Avenue
Boston: Prudential Center, 800 Boylston Street
Brookline: 2 Brookline Place
Needham: 110 Second Avenue
781-429-1500 | www.isismaternity.com

I Isis Maternity is one of the area's best parenting resources, offering classes, support groups, and retail in four locations in Boston and its

---

☼ Words of Wisdom

Isis Maternity, with four locations in the Boston area, is a rich resource for parents, offering numerous classes and support groups. Great Beginnings, for first-time moms and infants up to age ten weeks, is one of their core classes and is immensely popular. President and CEO Johanna McChesney weighs in on why getting out of the house and making new connections is vital.

"New parenthood is not easy. Having a baby can be very isolating. People live away from traditional support these days, and you don't have a Rolodex of people who just had a baby," says McChesney, who calls the new moms groups an instant community. "The support is unbelievable. It's very emotional. You see nine other people going through the same thing. You don't have to be intimidated to breastfeed or let your flabby belly hang out."

Her tips for having a successful group: "Open up and welcome these new people in your life. Share your stories. Don't be judgmental. And don't worry about germs!"

surrounding neighborhoods. Purchasing a membership (which is a bargain—$66 for one year; $42 for six months) gives you great discounts on all of what Isis offers, but you don't have to join to enjoy their programs. For more information on classes, see chapter 2. For information on their play groups, see chapter 6. Different programs are offered at different sites and are always being added. Check the Isis website for current schedules.

Great Beginnings
For moms with babies two to ten weeks old at the start of group. You can register prenatally. Select a class that starts four weeks after your due date.
Six-week session. Check website for dates.
Cost: $179 ($161.10 for members).

These expert-led, one-and-a-half-hour weekly meetings offer support, information, and discussion. Topics covered include feeding and sleeping patterns, establishing routines and patterns, soothing fussiness and gas, returning to work, child care choices, and much more. Infant massage and developmental play activities are introduced each week to explore nurturing new ways to entertain and interact with your baby. A group like this is a great way to share your experiences and find some camaraderie.

Time for Dads
For fathers and their babies (newborn to pre-crawlers).
Four-week session. Check website for dates.
Cost: $130 ($117 for members).

Similar to the new moms' groups, dads learn about infant development and safety and discuss parenting topics. Moms aren't the only ones who should get out to make new friends—and dads can do just that during these seventy-five-minute weekly sessions.

Twins New Moms Group
For mothers and twin babies age one to four months. Triplets are welcome.
Six-week session. Check website for dates.
Cost: $179 ($161.10 for members).

Hang out in an environment where two babies (or more) is the norm and join other moms of multiples. Share tips and tricks to get you through your exhausting, exhilarating first few months. A facilitator (a mom of twins) will lead talks and give ideas for your babies' health, development, feeding, and sleep.

Jewish Family & Children's Service
1430 Main Street, Waltham
781-647-5327 | www.jfcsboston.org
Free.

⊞ Jewish Family & Children's Service provides a range of human service and healthcare programs, guided by Jewish traditions of social responsibility, compassion, and respect for all members of the community. It's worth noting that you don't need to be Jewish to use their excellent services.

They offer a number of new mom support groups throughout Massachusetts. Boston-area groups are listed below. The weekly sessions are for mothers of babies (newborn to one year) to help you begin to build a community. They also offer special themes such as Mothers of Twins, Triplets and More, Gay & Lesbian New Parents Group, and a postpartum adjustment group called This Isn't What I Expected. Visit their website to check the calendar.

Brookline
Temple Ohabei Shalom
1187 Beacon Street
Monday, 11AM–12:30PM

Cambridge
Congregation Eitz Chayim
134-136 Magazine Street
Wednesday, 10AM–11:30AM

Jamaica Plain
St. John's Church
1 Roanoke Avenue (at Revere Street)
Tuesday, 10AM–11:30AM

Newton
Temple Shalom
175 Temple Street
Monday, 11AM–12:30PM

Somerville
Somerville Family Network
42 Prescott Street (Cummings School)
Thursday, 11AM–12:30PM

 Crib Sheet

New parents are usually in danger of some sort of sleep deprivation in the early days. Sleep expert Dr. Richard Ferber, author of *Solve Your Child's Sleep Problems,* shares a few pointers.

- After the first couple of months, infants and parents should be on a fairly regular schedule.
- Parents should decide the circumstances the child will be sleeping under, whether it be a crib, a family bed, or so on. That's how the child should sleep, and it shouldn't change.
- Usually children will make it clear how much sleep they need. Usually parents are aiming for more sleep than is possible.
- People have strong tendencies to sleep in on weekends. If we let our children sleep later on the weekend and holidays, they will have trouble waking up on weekdays.
- In a nutshell: Be consistent. A good policy in most things!

Dr. Ferber is currently the Director of the Center for Pediatric Sleep Disorders at Children's Hospital Boston, which was established in 1978 as the world's first comprehensive center dedicated to the diagnosis and treatment of sleep disorders in children.

Massachusetts General Hospital—Vincent Obstetrics and Gynecology Services

32 Fruit Street, Boston
617-726-4312 | www.massgeneral.org; Search: New Moms Group
Tuesdays, 10AM–11:30AM, except for holiday weeks. Call to
pre-register.
Free.

I The Me and My Baby Support Group is a chance for you to meet other new mothers and professional leaders. Nurses and lactation consultants lead each group. Ask questions, share experiences, make friends, get support, and acquire breastfeeding support and education.

Parent Connection

Beth Israel Deaconess Medical Center
617-667-2229 | www.bidmc.org; Search: Parent Connection

I A free service for first-time parents who deliver here.

St. Margaret's Center for Women and Infants at Caritas St. Elizabeth

736 Cambridge Street, Brighton
617-562-7007 | www.semc.org; Search: Maternity Services

I Breastfeeding and support groups for mothers.

Ask Around the Playground!

Living in a tech-savvy city like Boston has its advantages. Almost all the communities in the Boston area have their own online groups. One of the most widely accessed groups is probably GardenMoms. A few years back, a group of South End moms founded this online group—now it's over a thousand members strong, serves parents from around Boston, and provides great resources by way of searchable archives. If you have questions—from swaddling to stroller recommendations—you can be sure it's come up on GardenMoms.

To apply for access to the list, go to www.gardenmoms.findsmithgroups. com. Similar resources exist for other Boston neighborhoods and Greater Boston suburbs. Ask the moms you see at the playground if they know of them (it's a great ice breaker) and log on!

The Birth Place

3 West, Menino Pavilion, Boston Medical Center
840 Harrison Avenue, Boston
617-414-4363 | www.bmc.org/pediatrics

I Services offered include breastfeeding classes, infant massage classes, mental healthcare and recovery from addiction, and pediatric and maternal follow-up care.

Barely Beyond Boston: Support Groups Outside the City Limits

Cambridge Women's Health Center

1493 Cambridge Street, Cambridge
617-665-2300 | www.cha.harvard.edu

I Offers services such as pediatrics, nursery care, childbirth education, lactation consultation, and postpartum care, among others.

Center for Families

Peabody School
70 Rindge Avenue, Cambridge
617-349-6385 | www.cambridgema.gov; Search: Center for Families
Free.

A The Center for Families is a family support program that serves families of children up to age six in Cambridge. They offer a variety of programs and are a great community resource. Newsletters on their website provide information on that month's activities.

Babytime: Caring, Playing, Nurturing

Peabody School
70 Rindge Avenue, Cambridge
Monday, 12:30PM–2:30PM

Margaret Fuller Neighborhood House
71 Cherry Street, Cambridge
Tuesday, 12:30PM–2:30PM

I This is an informal group (pick either Monday or Tuesday) for parents or caregivers with infants under fifteen months that offers the opportunity to share experiences, ask questions, and meet others. A light snack for adults is provided. The facilitator is a lactation counselor and infant massage instructor with a background as a nurse-midwife.

New Dad Class

Cambridge Hospital
1493 Cambridge Street, Cambridge
617-665-1662 | 617-665-1386
Classes are held on various Saturdays

ℹ️ New dads, like new moms, have lots of questions about how to provide the best care to their newborns. Patrick McDonagh, RN, and Kate Reist, CNM, Lactation Consultant, will discuss newborn care, feeding, and dad issues.

Harvard Vanguard Medical Associates

1611 Cambridge Street, Cambridge
617-661-5500 | www.vanguardmed.org
For current patients.

ℹ️ Offers health and wellness classes for parents, such as Caring for Your Newborn, which covers the routine care of infants and breastfeeding.

Newton Mothers' Forum

617-332-3632 | www.newtonmoms.com
Annual membership: $165.

🅰️ A non-profit organization created to help mothers in Newton and the surrounding areas meet and get to know each other, share ideas and information, and build a community for themselves and their families. There is a Meal for New Moms program, Mom's Night Out, playgroups, and special events.

Newton-Wellesley Hospital

2014 Washington Street (Route 16), Newton
617-243-6000 | www.nwh.org; Search: Childbirth Education
For current patients.

ℹ️ Newton-Wellesley Hospital offers programs and classes during pregnancy and throughout the early parenting period.

Sostek Home Care

379 Elliot Street, Suite 100H, Newton
617-244-8560 | www.sostekhomecare.com
$200–$285 per day (for one baby), plus a $45 one-time service fee.

ℹ️ Offers 24-hour, live-in care to provide postpartum assistance, newborn care, and breastfeeding support.

The MOMS Club of Brookline

www.momsclub.org; Search: Chapter Links
Annual membership: $30.

A A chapter of MOMS (Moms Offering Moms Support) Club International. The goal of the organization is to provide a support group for mothers who choose to stay at home to raise their children. MOMS hosts park days, playgroups, activity groups, group outings, family days, holiday parties, and Mom's Night Out.

The Rice Center for Young Children and Families at the Boston Institute for Psychotherapy

1415 Beacon Street, Brookline
617-566-2200 | www.bostoninstitute.org/rice.shtml

A Aims to support parents and children through their first five years together.

WarmLines Parent Resources

225 Nevada Street, Newtonville
617-244-INFO | www.warmlines.org
Free and fee-based programming.

I WarmLines was my bridge to the brand-new world of parenthood. They offer loads of information by connecting parents to each other and to resources in the community. Many programs are free, but those that are not free are still invaluable. For $60 you can get help with child care recommendations; when your child is older, access to the comprehensive summer camp connection (a database) for $40 might be just the ticket. WarmLines also offers music classes (see chapter 2) and special events throughout the year.

The programs below are both free and priceless:

New Babies/New Moms
This is a daytime group for first-time moms with babies up to six months that meets for six weeks. The ongoing program is offered year-

American Baby Care
617-504-8975 | www.americanbabycare.com
Fees vary with services
A baby concierge in Boston provides listings of private support counselors, safety, and exercise counselors, as well as parent educators who have designed many in-home classes, like infant massage. They also have a Diaper Diva service that provides an overnight infant care specialist.

Boston Mamas
www.bostonmamas.com
Online resource for moms and families in Boston.

Expectant Mothers Guide
www.expectantmothersguide.com
Find local resources for expecting and new mothers.

round, and you sign up according to your newborn's age. All the babies in the group will have been born within two or three weeks of each other, so every mom is on the same page. A professional facilitator keeps the conversation going and provides themes to talk about. You'll discuss developmental issues, expectations, changing relationships, child care options, and much more. Don't be surprised if you form lasting bonds with some of the other moms.

New Babies/New Parents Group
Similar to the above program, but it meets at night for eight weeks and is for first-time moms and/or dads with babies up to six months. It's offered in the spring and fall.

More Resources

LACTATION CONSULTANTS

Lactation Care Inc.
25 Fisher Avenue, Newton
617-244-5593 | www.lactationcare.com
Private breastfeeding classes: $85.

A small, women-owned business, founded to provide support and solutions for breastfeeding difficulties. Classes and products offered.

Tufts Medical Center, 750 Washington Street, Boston
617-636-0175 | www.tuftsmedicalcenter.org
$35 per couple.

800-LA-LECHE | 617-323-3467 | www.lalecheleague.org
Membership is $40, but many services are free and open to nonmembers.

Telephone counseling on breastfeeding, new mothers' groups, and information on breast pump rentals and sales. Some chapters will even come to your home to help. If your child isn't latching on properly—ouch—call in La Leche!

NIGHT NURSES

781-690-6776 | www.newbornnurses.org
Fees vary, call for details.

Registered nurses or experienced nannies come into your home and help you care for your baby through breastfeeding advice, postpartum assistance, and general night nurses.

POSTPARTUM DEPRESSION

Simches Research Building, 185 Cambridge Street,
Suite 2200, Boston
617-724-7792 | www.womensmentalhealth.org
Fees vary with insurance.

The Center for Women's Mental Health at Massachusetts General Hospital provides evaluations and treatment of psychiatric disorders.

The Center for Early Relationship Support at Jewish Family and Children's Service of Greater Boston

1430 Main Street, Waltham
781-647-5327 | www.jfcsboston.org
Fees vary with insurance.

Visiting Moms is for women who are pregnant or have children under one year and are struggling to cope with the expanding family.

Postpartum Support International

800-944-4PPD | www.postpartum.net

Postpartum Support International (PSI) was founded in 1987. The purpose of the organization is to increase awareness among public and professional communities about the emotional changes that women experience during pregnancy and postpartum. Approximately 15 percent of all women will experience postpartum depression following the birth of a child. The organization has a volunteer coordinator in every state and in twenty-six countries. PSI disseminates information and resources through volunteer coordinators, the website, and an annual conference.

Room to Grow

617-859-4545 | www.roomtogrow.org

This great organization provides parents in need with support and essential items through their child's first three years of life. Parents visit Room to Grow every three months, beginning in their third trimester. Social workers monitor the baby's development and help parents with all the ups and downs of those first years. At each visit, parents receive age-appropriate clothes, toys, books, and gear. If you're lucky enough not to need the services of Room to Grow, perhaps you'll consider assisting them in their mission: Room to Grow gladly accepts new and nearly new items. If you're looking for something to do with all the beautiful baby outfits your little one outgrew before she wore them, you have found your solution!

The Online PPD Support Group

www.ppdsupportpage.com

Offers information, support, and assistance for those dealing with postpartum mood disorders.

2 Classes & Gyms (for Grown-Ups)

WITH THE VARIETY of "mommy and me" classes offered in and around Boston, it's easy to get out of the house and have some fun. (Though keep in mind that these classes aren't *just* for mommies!) Classes are a

great way for parents to learn how to "play" again—and today's parents, who juggle hectic schedules, occasionally need a refresher course in this vital skill. These classes will also continue to widen your community, introduce you to neighborhood families, and expose your child to the amazing world around them.

The odds are that from the time your child is a few months old until she is ready for school, you'll try all sorts of classes. But parent-children classes don't have to end there—weekend classes for parents and school-age kids are a great way to block out some special time together.

When your baby is little, consider starting with a music class or a baby sign language class. Maybe when your little angel goes mobile, you'll want to sign up for a movement class. Before you know it, your son or daughter will be talking a blue streak—so why not learn a second language together? The offerings are diverse and plentiful, with many organizations, such as Isis Maternity, scheduling a variety of choices that range from movement to art.

A few words of caution, however. Don't overbook yourself or your child. With the amount on offer, you could easily participate in a class each day of the week or schedule all your preschooler's free time. Make sure you and your child are both interested in the class before you sign up for any long-term commitments. Keep in mind that many organizations will allow you to preview the class before asking you to fork over the credit card.

Of course, it can't all be fun and games. You may want to spend some time at the gym working off those pregnancy pounds. At the end of the chapter, you'll also find a comprehensive list of gyms that offer daycare.

General Parent & Baby Classes

Hill House
74 Joy Street, Boston
617-227-5838 | www.hillhouseboston.org

A This Beacon Hill non-profit community center, founded in 1966, offers everything from summer camps and cool after-school programs (think fencing!) to team sports and private music instruction. While most programs are geared toward toddlers and up, there are free playgroups (registration required) and a slew of music programs for older babies, six months and up. It's a fantastic and inexpensive resource for the city. Visit their website for the extensive list of programming available.

Isis Maternity
Arlington: 397 Massachusetts Avenue
Boston: Prudential Center, 800 Boylston Street
Brookline: 2 Brookline Place
Needham: 110 Second Avenue
781-429-1500 | www.isismaternity.com

A Isis Maternity is a new mom's mecca. The list of classes Isis offers is simply too long to detail here, but some of the perennial favorites include Movers & Groovers, a class for parents and babies nine to eleven months, which includes a welcome circle with songs, movement, finger play, infant sign language, and more. Itsy Bitsy Toddler Yoga is another popular class—you and your little crawler (up to age two) will explore over seventy-five poses, songs, and activities designed by a baby-yoga expert. And then there is Bouncin' Joeys, a forty-five-minute creative movement class for kids age 2 to 2.11 years with a parent.

But this is just the tip of the iceberg. Isis offers parent/child classes for a variety of ages and interests. Visit their website for a full roster.

♛ Great Children's Consignment Shops

Kids outgrow their clothes almost as soon as you buy them. Pick up great deals at local children's consignment shops, as well as toys, books, and equipment.

Children's Orchard
807 Boylston Street, Brookline
617-277-3006 | www.childrensorchard.com
Gently-used and new kid's clothing, toys, furniture, equipment, books, and accessories are available. I love to buy used ice skates here because they are already broken in, which makes both my daughter and me happy. When she was a baby and outgrowing clothes every five minutes, I often sold them here, along with toys and books she no longer used.

Kid to Kid
42 Worcester Street, Natick
508-650-4001 | www.natick.kidtokid.com
Definitely worth the drive, Kid to Kid offers both new and used clothes in fantastic shape, plus equipment, books, toys, and shoes. They also carry maternity clothes.

Pink Dolly
8 Medford Street, Arlington
781-646-7811 | www.insideandcompany.com
This store has a fairly strict policy on what it accepts, so you won't see Target, Kohl's, or Kids-R-Us brands, but you will find Oilily, Cake Walk, Hanna Anderson, Zutano, Stride Rite, Mulberry Bush, Baby Lulu, and Gap. They also have maternity clothes.

Mama & Me

284 Amory Street, Jamaica Plain
617-372-7448 | www.mymamaandme.com

A Mama & Me offers a variety of interactive classes and programs for toddlers and their parents (not just mamas). Their space is completely green, with bamboo floors, nontoxic paints, and organic materials. Drop in for an art class or boogie with your baby in a dance class. Also check out the preschool prep program, which gets toddlers ready for their next big step.

Movement Classes

Boston Ballet

Boston Studio: 19 Clarendon Street | 617-695-6950
MetroWest Studio: 863 Washington Street, Newtonville | 617-456-6263
South Shore Studio: 34 Accord Park Drive, Norwell | 617-456-6273 or 781-871-7468
North Shore Studio: Lynch/van Otterloo YMCA, 40 Leggs Hill Road, Marblehead | 617-456-6380
www.bostonballet.org

T There are a variety of options for children at Boston Ballet at four different locations. The youngest kids can enroll in the Hand 'n Hand program, designed to introduce children age two to dancing with one parent or caregiver. There are boys-only classes, creative dance, rhythm, ballet, and many other options. All classes in the children's program meet once a week from September to June, with ongoing enrollment through June of the school year, provided space is available. Call or visit the website for details and fees.

Brookline Ballet School

1431 Beacon Street, Brookline (Coolidge Corner)
617-879-9988 | www.brooklineballet.com

A Age-appropriate dance and exercise options are available for children and parents, including parent/child Pilates and yoga, rhythmic gymnastics, and pre-ballet, which prepares children for the school's formal Youth Ballet and other dance programs. Check the website for details and schedules. Short-term daycare can be arranged nearby while parents are in class.

Charles River Aquatics

Boston University's Case Center Pool
285 Babcock Street, Boston
617-777-3556 | www.charlesriveraquatics.com

A Half-hour Tiny Tots classes are offered for parents and children ages six months to three years. When your little swimmer is ready, they move up to Level 1 classes, where they can learn to blow bubbles underwater and begin to learn age-appropriate swimming skills. One catch though—all swimmers in Level 1 and up must be potty-trained.

Fresh Pond Ballet

1798A Massachusetts Avenue, Cambridge
617-491-5865 | www.freshpondballet.com

T Introduce your tiny dancer of two or three years to movement, co-ordination, and balance in classes especially designed for children. Children four years and up can enroll in pre-ballet classes in this intimate studio. Parents don't have to dance, but are expected to stay during classes.

Green Street Studios

185 Green Street, Cambridge
617-864-3191 | www.greenstreetstudios.org

A Green Street is a center for movement and dance. It offers parent/child classes for children ages two to four years, as well as Music Together for newborns and their parents.

Gymboree

109 Oak Street, Newton
617-244-2988 | www.gymboreeclasses.com

A Gymboree, an old-timer in the world of parent/baby classes, offers a variety of programming that ranges from music to sports to art, with a focus on kids from birth to age five. You and your tot will have fun singing, playing with instruments, tumbling, or just playing around in general—something most adults need more of!

Gymnastic Academy of Boston
128 Smith Place, Cambridge
617-441-9700 | www.gymnasticacademyofboston.com

P The academy offers preschool and kindergarten classes. Tumbling tots as young as three years can participate. The academy maintains a low student to teacher ratio (8:1). They ask that gymnastics be viewed as a year-long commitment, so that your child has enough time to develop all the skills gymnastics classes will teach them. Check the website for class schedules.

Joanne Langione Dance Center
35 Border Street, West Newton
617-969-8724 | www.jldancecenter.com

T Dancin' with Mommy introduces children ages twenty months through two-and-a-half to the endless possibilities of movement and dance. Playdance, for kids ages two through four, encourages love of music and movement, and ensures that young children do not begin formal training too early. Introduction to Dance is offered to kids ages 3.9 to 5 to develop coordination and movement.

Mommy & Baby Yoga
Wellness Center at the Newton-Wellesley Hospital
2014 Washington Street (Route 16), Newton
617-243-6221

I This class is designed to help new moms reduce stress and improve overall health and well-being, while connecting with their new babies and meeting other new moms.

My Gym
Various Locations
www.my-gym.com

A Channel your child's inner athlete with a fitness class—or just get him to burn off some extra energy! Age-appropriate fitness groups are designed for children as young as six weeks. Classes help foster a healthy relationship between your child and physical activity. Check the website for locations and schedules.

StrollerFit

Various locations
617-429-6369 | www.strollerfit.com

A Like Music Together, this franchise trains instructors and sets them loose on the community. Instructors hold aerobic certifications from nationally accredited agencies and must attain a special StrollerFit Certification before they can become authorized to teach group fitness classes. Parents can exercise with children at a variety of indoor and outdoor spaces depending on the season. In the Boston area, a class might be held at the Arnold Arboretum in nice weather or a community center in cold weather. Visit the website for details.

The Green Planet

22 Lincoln Street, Newton Highlands
617-332-7841

T A neighborhood yoga studio and creative center, the Green Planet offers children's yoga classes periodically. Call for details.

The Little Gym

1208B VFW Parkway, West Roxbury
617-323-9769 | www.thelittlegym.com

A Children from infants to three years attend classes with a parent/caregiver. Activities include aerobics, elementary gymnastics skills, stretching, rhythm, songs, group activities, ball play, and bubbles. Classes for different age groups are offered Monday through Saturday.

Tony Williams Dance Center

284 Amory Street, Jamaica Plain
617-524-4381 | www.tonywilliamsdancecenter.com

T TWDC offers an array of classes for children, from First Steps, a ballet class for kids ages three to four, to jazz, tap, and hip-hop classes.

United South End Settlements

48 Rutland Street, South End
617-375-8150 | www.uses.org

A United South End Settlements is a neighborhood gem, offering two physical activity classes for infants and toddlers, plus a variety of other classes for preschoolers, from Yoga to Family Music Makers to Spanish and Creative Movement. Caretakers are expected to participate in the class with the children. Classes meet once a week and last for eight weeks.

YMCA
Various locations (see page 39)
www.ymcaboston.org

A The YMCA of Greater Boston is one of the largest urban Ys in the U.S.; it was also the first, founded in 1851. Modeled on the original YMCA established in London in 1844, the organization offered a safe gathering place for socializing and study. Over the years, its mission evolved to improve body, mind, and spiritual health for all. Today, it is the largest

---

☸ Learn a Second Language!

ABC: Spanish in Motion
Various locations
617-676-7680 | www.ABCSpanishInMotion.com
Spanish songs and games introduce wee ones to a world of different cultures. Classes are held in Belmont, Jamaica Plain, South End, Winchester, Dedham, and West Roxbury.

Greek 4 Kids
1345 Centre Street, Newton
617-953-9092 | www.greek-4-kids.com
Children six months and up of any heritage receive an exciting introduction to the Greek language—students can take pride that it's not all Greek to them!

LINX
141 Linden Street, Wellesley
781-235-3210 | www.linx-usa.com
Kids as young as eighteen months learn Spanish through the use of props, toys, and role-play. LINX also offers Mandarin for kindergarten-age kids.

The French Library Alliance Française of Boston
53 Marlborough Street, Boston
617-912-0400 | www.frenchlib.org
The Bébé Alliance class uses nursery rhymes, games, and music to introduce children six months to two years to the French language. Alliance Enfant, for children age three and up, uses music and flash cards to begin a child's learning of letters and numbers.

provider of after-school programs and child care in the Commonwealth. There are simply far too many programs to list here, so visit the website to find swimming, art, movement, and other exciting classes.

Music Classes

Baby Wiggle
Boston Center for the Arts
527 Tremont Street, South End
617-823-3010 | www.babywiggle.com

A Those who have participated in Baby Wiggle rave about it, and founder Sara Wheeler is a veritable celebrity amongst the youngest set of Bostonians. These lively music classes are designed to help infants and toddlers interact through sound, sight, and touch using drums, shakers, tambourines, puppets, bubbles, balls, and one exciting, extra-large parachute. All Baby Wiggle teachers hold music degrees specializing in Music Education or Music Therapy. Families receive a song book with lyrics and a CD to use at home. Parents or guardians must accompany their child and participate in the music class.

Brookline Music School
25 Kennard Road, Brookline
617-277-4593 | www.bmsmusic.org

P Offers various music and movement classes for kids four months and up with a parent or caregiver. Classes focus on stimulating social, emotional, and physical development. For children ages three to five years, ballet and dance classes are offered, as well as flute classes.

Community Music Center Boston
34 Warren Avenue, South End
617-482-7494 | www.cmcb.org

A Now in its ninety-ninth year, CMCB is an accredited non-profit music school. They serve more than five thousand students each week, both on-site in the Boston Center for the Arts and in nearly fifty community sites each year, including more than twenty Boston Public Schools. They offer early childhood classes for children as young as five months old with a caregiver and continue on up through age eight. In addition, there are private and group classes for virtually every instrument available. Call for schedules and prices.

Family Music Makers
Various locations
617-783-9818 | www.familymusicmakers.com

A This is a program designed for children from newborn through seven years old. The Little Music Makers classes are all mixed ages (so you can bring your other kids). Kidstompers is for kids ages three to five, and Kidservatory is a musical theater program for ages four to seven years. Classes are held in a variety of preschools, community centers, and church spaces. This is a fun and easy way to introduce your kids to the world of music through a variety of genres—from jazz to folk to rock.

Kindermusik
Various locations
www.kindermusik.com

A Kindermusik provides music and movement education to children newborn to age seven. There are a variety of classes for children and their caregivers. Classes are held at various Isis Maternity locations, yoga studios, community centers, and other spots. Visit the website to find schedules and prices.

Let's Make Music at WarmLines
225 Nevada Street, Newtonville
617-244-INFO | www.warmlines.org

A WarmLines offers a multi-age program for children and their adult partners. The forty-five-minute class features songs, finger play, and movement using a variety of rhythm instruments and materials. Songs incorporate elements of traditional and contemporary children's music. The class is followed by a thirty-minute informal playtime with age-appropriate toys.

Longy School of Music
1 Follen Street, Cambridge
617-876-0956 | www.longy.edu

T The Longy School of Music is internationally recognized for its Dalcroze Eurhythmics programs. Longy offers specialized Dalcroze programs to children as young as twelve months, as well as music and movement classes for children and caretakers. Early Beginning classes help develop coordination and singing ability for children three years and older, to be attended by a caregiver as well. The Stepping Stones class encourages motor development and musical creativity.

Music Together

Various locations
800-728-2692 | www.musictogether.com

A This early childhood music program franchise has classes for babies, toddlers, preschoolers, and kindergarteners with an adult. They are often held in conjunction with other schools or programs, but are all taught by certified Music Together teachers. Check out the website to find a class near you.

The Children's Music Center of Jamaica Plain

The Brewery Complex
284 Amory Street, Jamaica Plain
617-524-1784 | www.jamaicaplainmusic.com

A The center provides music education for children of all ages. Music Together allows children six months to five years to explore music in a playful, non-performance environment. Children learn by moving with the music, playing instruments, and watching adults sing. Classes meet weekly for forty-five minutes. Two CDs, a songbook, and a parent guide are included in the enrollment fee.

Baby Can Dance!

Baby Loves Disco, a brilliant idea dreamed up by a mom in Philly about five years ago, transforms hipster nightclubs into afternoon party havens for kids and their parents. About once a month in cities across the country (including Boston), real DJs spin music from the '70s and '80s (no Raffi or Barney, thank you very much), which gets everyone up and moving. In Boston, the fun happens on Sundays from 2pm–5pm at the Revolution Rock Bar (200 High Street, Boston). In addition to dancing, there might be bubble machines, baskets of scarves and egg-shakers, a chill-out room with tents, books, and puzzles, diaper-changing stations, and healthy snacks. Check the website, www.babylovesdisco.com and reserve early! These events sell out faster than you can say Boogie Ooggie Ooggie!

Arts & Education Classes

Arlington Center for the Arts
Gibbs Center, 41 Foster Street, Arlington
781-648-6220 | www.acarts.org

P The Arlington Center for the Arts was established as a community arts center in 1988 by a group of artists, writers, musicians, and educators. It offers more than 250 programs annually in the visual, literary, and performing arts, many of which are free. There are any number of classes for children in grades K–5, from drumming to mixed media, plus a few family classes for adults and kids as young as three. Visit the website or call for schedules and fees, which are unbelievably reasonable.

Artbeat
212A Massachusetts Avenue, Arlington
781-646-2200 | www.artbeatonline.com
Sunday, noon–6PM; Monday–Wednesday, 10AM–6PM; Thursday–Saturday, 10AM–8PM.
Fees vary.

P This fantastic art studio is filled with paints, papers, glitter, glass, ceramic tiles, colored sand, and any other material your little Picasso could want to create his masterpiece. During store hours, you and your child can walk in and choose from a variety of art projects. There are also special projects offered every Saturday for kids ages four and up with an adult. Check the website for what's doing the week you want to go.

Boston Children's Theatre
321 Columbus Avenue, Boston
617-424-6634 | www.bostonchildrenstheatre.org

P Think you have a budding starlet on your hands? Check out the BCT's class, Centerstage Discovery. This introduction to creative drama for kids four to seven-years-old is taught by a theater-education specialist. Classes meet Saturday mornings for four weeks ($125) and include drama games, activities, and crafts based on seasonal themes. At the end of the session, parents are invited to a "sharing session." The BCT offers classes and workshops for children and teenagers up to age eighteen. For more information on their performances, see chapter 3.

Brookline Arts Center

86 Monmouth Street, Brookline
617-566-5715 | www.brooklineartscenter.com

P The Brookline Arts Center offers moms, dads, and tots classes during the week, along with parent and child pottery classes for children three to five years. For children four and older there are drawing and painting classes, as well as a Bookworm class, where kids create art based on favorite children's books.

Create a Cook

53 Winchester Street, Newton
617-795-2223 | www.createacook.com

P The Petite Fours classes are offered to preschoolers, ages three to five years, and their caregiver. These tiny aspiring chefs are introduced to cooking and baking skills, as well as how to count and measure ingredients. Basic kitchen safety is built into the class recipe. Classes are divided into seven, five-week terms.

New England Aquarium

Central Wharf, Boston
617-973-5200 | www.neaq.org

T The aquarium offers several classes for the child interested in aquatic life. Family Explorers introduces young children to the submarine world and encourages the early science skills of observation and exploration. This hour-long class is offered for toddlers, two-year-olds, and preschoolers (three to four years of age) in a series of four classes. The Little Fishes Program is offered to parents and one-year-olds as a six-week series.

Puddlestompers

86 Hawthorne Avenue, Needham
781-449-0776 | www.puddlestompers.com

T Discover the mysteries of nature with your child. These age-appropriate classes based on seasonal themes may include exploring animal habitats or "bug hunting." Designed to connect kids with the world around them, these classes are sure to be a great hit. Each session ends with a snack and a story related to the day's theme. Conducted on publicly owned land in Brookline, Wellesley, and Needham, sessions are eight weeks long and correspond to the four seasons. (Yes, even winter!) Each weekly class runs fifty-five minutes and is limited to ten adult/child pairs per group. The fun moves indoors in bad weather.

Riverside Theatre Works

45 Fairmount Avenue, Hyde Park
617-361-7024 | www.riversidetheatreworks.org

A In addition to offering several family-friendly shows a year, this non-profit performing arts center's mission is to provide affordable arts education. The offerings are diverse and wonderful—a veritable embarrassment of riches. Try Mommy, Music and Me! ($145/ten-week session), which uses music and stories from different cultures to get parents, infants, and toddlers inspired. Kids ages three to five can participate in the early childhood creative drama program, Riverside Tots ($350/year; one hour a week), while children age four and up can try Creative Dramatics ($300/year), which meets once a week for forty-five minutes and includes singing, dancing, instrument play, and turning stories into plays. Another class for kids four and up is Funky Folktales ($145). During this beginning acting class, students bring folktales to life in their own unique, funky way. Parents and friends are invited to see the end result during the last day of class. This is just the tip of the iceberg, though. Simply visit the website to find a music, theater, or dance class that is perfect for you and your child—whatever his age!

The Children's Art Centre at United South End Settlements

48 Rutland Street, South End
617-375-8150 | www.childrensartcentre.blogspot.com

P It's worth mentioning again: USES offers a vast amount of programming for infants through school-age children, but the Children's Art Center—located in a sun-filled studio adjacent to the main building—is a hidden treasure. In Creative Art preschoolers explore three different art projects all centered around a single, weekly theme. In Story Art, children take inspiration from children's literature to create their own masterpieces.

61 Washington Park, Newtonville
617-964-3424 | www.newartcenter.org

P The New Art Center is a non-profit community art center. It offers a weekend clay class for parents and prekindergarten children to develop imaginative thinking—and get their hands a little dirty!

Gyms with Child Care

More often than not, if a gym has the space, they'll offer some sort of child care. Many are for specific hours only and often book up fast. Usually you'll need to bring your own diapers, wipes, snacks, and a change of clothes. Some spots will change diapers; others will page you. Once you get into a groove, you and your child will be able to figure out the best time to squeeze in a workout. Make sure you call ahead in case the center is full or hours have changed.

Benefitness Health Club for Women

62 Harvard Street, Brookline
617-232-7440 | www.benefitnesshealthclub.com
Ages: 3 months–9 years
Call for hours
$8 for one-and-a-half hours ($12 for two children); pre-booking is required.

If your child needs a diaper change, a bottle, or is crying and upset, the staff will find you.

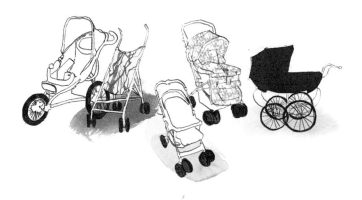

Boston Athletic Club

653 Summer Street, Boston
617-269-4300 | www.bostonathleticclub.com
Ages: 3 months–10 years
Call for hours
$5 per hour for members; $6 for nonmembers.

The BAC offers a nice block of time to for parents to work out, since they'll watch kids for up to three hours.

Boston Sports Club

Various locations
www.mysportsclubs.com
Ages: 3 months–10 years
Prices and hours vary with the club. Call your location for details.

BSC will watch kids in their playroom for two hours, but they usually won't change diapers, so be prepared to be paged if your baby needs a clean-up.

Equinox Fitness Club

131 Dartmouth Street, Back Bay
617-578-8918 | www.equinoxfitness.com
Ages: Over 3 months
Call for hours.

Gold's Gym

323 Dorchester Ave, South Boston
617-268-5500 | www.goldsgym.com

Child care in Arlington, West Roxbury, Natick, and Needham (Needham has partnership with Isis Maternity) locations.

Healthworks Fitness Centers for Women

Back Bay: 411 Stuart Street | 617-859-7700
Brookline: 1300 Boylston Street | 617-383-6100
Brookline: 920 Commonwealth Avenue | 617-731-3030
Cambridge: 36 White Street, Porter Square | 617-497-4454
www.healthworksfitness.com
Ages: 6 weeks–8 years; varies slightly depending upon location.

Healthworks' Nursery has a time limit of two-and-a-half hours per visit.

Leventhal-Sidman Jewish Community Center Fitness Center

333 Nahanton Street, Newton
617-558-6457 | www.lsjcc.org
Ages: 3 months-10 years
Sunday-Friday, 8:30AM-noon; Saturday, 8AM-11:30AM (Coupons must be purchased in advance)

If your child needs a diaper change, a bottle, or is crying and upset, the staff will find you. You can pre-register and reserve your spot for a specific day and time by filling out the registration form.

The Sports Club/LA

4 Avery Street, Boston
617-375-8543 | www.thesportsclubla.com
Ages: 3 months-12 years
Daily, 8:30AM-1:30PM; Monday, Wednesday, Thursday, 3:30PM-7PM; Tuesday, 3:30PM-6PM
$9 per hour, two-hour maximum.

The nursery is overseen by early childhood specialists.

YMCA

Various locations listed below
www.ymcaboston.org

The Y can be one-stop shopping for all your fitness needs, for both you and your kids. Check out the website of the Y closest to you to see what's on offer. The hours given below are the hours of operation for the nurseries. Child care is free for members. There is a small fee for non-members.

Dorchester
776 Washington Street | 617-436-7750
Ages: 3 months-6 years
Monday-Friday, 6AM-9PM; Saturday, 9AM-noon

East Boston
215 Bremen Street | 617-569-9622
Ages: 3 months-6 years
Monday-Friday, 9:15AM-12:15PM and 5:15PM-7:15PM; Saturday, 9:15AM-12:15PM

Huntington Avenue
316 Huntington Avenue, Boston | 617-536-7800
Ages: 8 months–12 years
Monday and Wednesday, 5PM–8PM

Oak Square
615 Washington Street, Brighton | 617-782-3535
Ages: 6 weeks–10 years
Monday–Saturday, 9AM–noon; Sunday, 9AM–11:30AM; Monday–Thursday, 5PM–7:45PM

West Suburban YMCA
276 Church Street, Newton Corner
617-244-6050 | www.ymcainnewton.org
Ages: 3 months–10 years
Monday–Friday, 8:45AM–1PM and 3:30PM–5:30PM; Saturday, 9AM–1PM

Maximum time is ninety minutes per day per child.

3 Enriching Adventures in Boston

IT WOULD BE a crime not to introduce your child to all the amazing art, culture, and history Boston has to offer—and if you think a two-year-old

can't enjoy the opera, think again! Almost all of the city's theaters and orchestras offer family shows, sometimes even with children performing. Libraries are probably the richest resource around for free family fun. I have spent hours at almost all of the city's libraries for one activity or another, from story hours to puppet shows to author readings to free movies. All these events cater to children, proving that the city really is their oyster.

As for museums, don't limit yourself to just the Children's Museum and the Museum of Science (though you certainly shouldn't miss them!). Most of the museums in Boston have special programs for families, or at the very least a few child-friendly exhibits that will keep them occupied long enough for parents and caregivers to get a well-deserved dose of grown-up culture. Personally, I love the Museum of Fine Arts treasure hunt; the materials the museum provides are perfectly geared to help you and your child navigate such a large museum.

Boston is home to some of the richest history in the United States, and a great deal of that history is readily accessible to the youngest set. At first glance, some of the listings I have included may make you scratch your head, but trust me: even sites targeted for adults have something to offer little people, and I've included tips and tricks to make the most of those sites whenever possible. Someday in the not too distant future, that visit to Paul Revere's house will resonate with your child—maybe she'll be in fourth grade, maybe she'll be in college—but it will resonate and she will realize that she grew up surrounded by Boston's amazing history.

In addition to venue descriptions, you'll find age recommendations—but, again, take these for what they are worth. A mature toddler may enjoy the MIT Museum while a rambunctious five-year-old might find it a total bore; you know your child best. I've also tried to include membership information whenever possible, as this is a great way to save money. The overall benefit of having a yearly membership is that you'll be less attached to getting your money's worth out of one visit. I know moms who will pop into a museum for forty-five minutes or less because that is all their kids can handle. Ancillary benefits, such as discounted parking, reciprocity with other museums or zoos, or priority tickets might also appeal to you. Either way, when you're not worrying about wasting money, everyone will have a much better time. Later, you and your kids will remember these excursions as wonderful urban adventures when you discovered the city together!

Libraries

Boston Public Central Library

700 Boylston Street, Boston
617-536-5400 | www.bpl.org
Monday–Thursday, 9AM–9PM; Friday–Saturday, 9AM–5PM.
Free.

A Founded in 1848 and opened in 1854, the main branch is the granddaddy of Boston's libraries and was the first free library open to the public in the United States. The Rey Children's Room is a wonderful space that features story hours, puppet shows, sing-a-longs, and other special activities throughout the year. In addition to the main library, there are twenty-seven neighborhood branches, and there is always something going on at one of them. Visit the main website for calendar listings. Also, don't forget to see what free or discounted museum passes the library has—you can save a bundle that way. See page 86 for information on branch libraries.

Museums & Other Attractions

African Meeting House/Museum of African-American History

46 Joy Street, Boston
617-725-0022 | www.afroammuseum.org
Monday–Saturday, 10AM–4PM.
Free.

P America's oldest standing African-American church was built in 1806. It was an important nineteenth century center for the black community of Boston and was sometimes called Black Faneuil Hall. The New England Anti-Slavery Society was founded here in 1832. Check their website for wonderful special programs, including meeting children's book authors, actors portraying famous abolitionists, and Kwanzaa events.

Boston Children's Museum

300 Congress Street, Boston
617-426-8855 | www.bostonkids.org
Daily, 10AM–5PM; Friday until 9PM.
Adults, $10; children 2–15, $8; age 1, $2; under 1, free.
Friday nights are Family Dollar Night. Admission is $1 per person from 5PM to 9PM.
Family memberships are available from $125; caregivers can be added for an additional $10. Membership includes admission to additional children's museums around the country.

A In 2007, the museum underwent a complete renovation in order to become a green building. Numerous exhibits from the Art Studio to Arthur's Friends to the Construction Zone can keep kids entertained for hours. Head to the Playspace if you have children under age three and want to get away from the bigger kids for a while (open Saturday–Thursday, 10am–4:30pm; Friday, 10am–8:30pm). There's a tree house climber, a toy train landscape, and a cushioned infant area. The Family Resource Room offers parenting information and reading materials.

If you find that your family visits the museum all the time, consider a membership. This might be the best deal in town. Throughout the week the museum offers music, art, and cooking classes specifically for the younger set. Also, make sure you check the KidStage for pint-sized productions your toddler and preschooler are sure to enjoy. See the events calendar for more information.

Boston Fire Museum

344 Congress Street, Boston
617-482-1344 | www.bostonfiremuseum.com
May–November, Saturday, 11AM–4PM.
Free.

P Since most kids adore fire engines, a Saturday visit to see the antique fire equipment and photos in this 1891 firehouse could be considered as fun as going to a candy store. The museum, which formerly housed Engine Companies 38 and 39, and later Engine 39 and Ladder 18, even allows children to play with and climb on some of the equipment. Make sure you show your little one the jewel of the collection—a hand-drawn, hand-operated pumper put into service in 1793.

☆ Don't Pass This By!

You can pick up passes to various museums with just your local library card. Each library has a different allotment of passes. Scout your local library's website to find what they have.

Boston Public Library: www.bpl.org
Brookline Public Library: www.brooklinelibrary.org
Cambridge Public Library: www.ci.cambridge.ma.us/~cpl
Newton Free Library: www.newtonfreelibrary.net

Franklin Park Zoo

1 Franklin Park Road, Boston
617-541-5466 | www.zoonewengland.com
April–September, daily, 10AM–5PM; Saturday–Sunday until 6PM;
October–March, daily, 10AM–4PM.
Adults, $12; children 2–15, $7; under 2, free.

Half-price the first Saturday of the month between 10AM and noon.

Family memberships range from $70 to $100; memberships include free or discounted admission to 140 zoos around the country, including the five in Massachusetts.

A Lions, tigers, and giraffes—yes, the zoo has them all! In addition, the Franklin Farm exhibit is always a big hit with kids. Children can pet cows and goats and check out baby chicks. The Butterfly Landing, open only in the summer, has more than a thousand butterflies to gaze at in wonder. The Tropical Rainforest is home to seven lowland gorillas. Special events include the Zoo Howl in October, when kids can go along a trick-or-treat trail through the zoo, and sing-a-longs and other activities in the winter months.

Institute of Contemporary Art

100 Northern Avenue, Boston
617-478-3100 | www.icaboston.org
Tuesday, Wednesday, Saturday, and Sunday, 10AM–5PM; Thursday and Friday until 9PM.
Adults, $12; under 12, free.
Free on Thursdays after 5PM.
Free for families (up to two adults accompanied by children twelve and under) on the last Saturday of each month.
Family membership is $95; membership includes invitation to annual family event and discounts to family programs.

T Believe it or not, this gorgeous new museum is a wonderful spot to take the kids, especially for its Play Date program, held on the last Saturday of each month. Families get in free, and the entire day is packed with everything from films, performance, art-making activities, and gallery tours—all of which is tailored to an ongoing exhibit. Word to the wise: get there early! It can get very crowded. The setting on the waterfront is stunning. Kids will love running around outside and up and down the stairs while you watch the activity in the harbor.

Isabella Stewart Gardner Museum

280 The Fenway, Boston
617-566-1401 | www.gardnermuseum.org
Tuesday–Sunday, 11AM–5PM.
Adults, $12; under 18 or named Isabella, free.
If you visit the Gardner and the Museum of Fine Arts in a two-day period, you can get $2 off admission at either museum.

P The Gardner Museum is a time capsule museum, and it remains exactly as it was when Isabella Stewart Gardner died in 1924. It might not seem the best museum for kids, but pick up the family guides available at the information desk on your way in and you'll have intriguing rhymes to repeat, a treasure hunt, and culture all rolled into one. Check the website for the occasional family-themed events throughout the year, such as arts and crafts, period music concerts, and dance recitals.

John F. Kennedy Library and Museum

Columbia Point, Boston
617-514-1600 | www.jfklibrary.org
Daily, 9AM–5PM.
Adults, $10; children 13–17, $7; under 12, free.

P The John F. Kennedy Presidential Library and Museum portrays the life, leadership, and legacy of President Kennedy in a breathtaking waterfront location. A replica of the Oval Office is one of the exhibits dedicated to the thirty-fifth president. Although much of the museum's content is targeted for adults and older children, preschoolers may enjoy the mock-ups. In addition, a popular program for families is the Celebrate! arts series, which is offered about once a month. The free one-hour program focuses on arts, music, and culture.

Mapparium at the Christian Science Center

175 Huntington Avenue, Boston
617-450-3790 | www.marybakereddylibrary.org
Tuesday–Sunday, 10AM–4PM; closed major holidays.
Adults, $6; children 6–17, $4; under 6, free.
Fountain on in the summer, free.

T The Christian Science Publication Society Building looks daunting, but the huge complex on Massachusetts Avenue has a lot to offer children. Outside, toddlers and older kids love the enormous fountain (670 feet x 100 feet), and it's a happening place on a steamy summer day. But the beautiful Mapparium inside is just as enticing. Measuring thirty feet in diameter, the Mapparium is a gigantic stained glass globe that you can walk through. It's a look at world geography as it was in 1935. You can whisper to each other across the room and because of the acoustics it sounds like you are standing right next to each other. All in all, you're likely to spend only twenty minutes inside, but it is a special sight that offers kids a different perspective of the world.

Museum of Fine Arts

465 Huntington Avenue, Boston
617-267-9300 | www.mfa.org
Daily, 10AM–4:45PM;
Wednesday–Friday until 9:45PM.
(Only the West Wing is open late
Thursday and Friday; tickets are $2
less after 5PM.)

*Adults, $17; children 7–17, $6.50 until
3PM (after 3PM, free); under 6, free.*

*Your ticket allows you to visit twice
in a ten-day period. After 4PM on
Wednesday, admission is by voluntary
contribution.*

Family memberships start at $100.

T The Museum of Fine Arts (MFA) is huge and can be intimidating to the uninitiated and the very small. Rather than aimlessly dragging your kids around in an effort to find something that interests them, go online to download self-guided activity sheets (or pick one up at the information center). Depending on your child, you might choose Mythical Creatures or Cats, among other topics. Keep an eye open for the Family Art Cart on weekends from 11am to 4pm, when kids can learn about ancient Egyptian mysteries, read stories from Southeast Asia, or go through the museum with a set of Art Cards, looking for animals, treasures, and children in the artwork.

If you decide to head off on your own, it's a good idea to have a game plan in mind. Pick two or three exhibits that you want to visit, then call it quits. Nobody likes a cranky kid in a museum—especially mom and dad! The Egyptian Gallery is a no-brainer; kids always love the mummies. The Modern Art Gallery can make for interesting discussions with your young art critic. The Art of Africa Gallery fascinates children with beautiful masks.

Keep in mind that as your young ones grow, they can really take advantage of all the MFA has to offer. After-school programs, 3:30pm–4:45pm (weekdays only), for children ages six through twelve are available on a drop-in basis during the school year. Your future artist—or art historian—will explore the MFA's different galleries and do exciting and reflective projects with museum staff. The program is free—and to get your kids hooked on art for the rest of their lives is priceless!

Museum of Science

Science Park, Boston
617-723-2500 | www.mos.org
Daily, 9AM–5PM; Friday until 9PM; July–Labor Day, 9AM–7PM.
Adults, $19; children 3–11, seniors over 65, $16; under 3, free.
Mugar Omni Theater, Planetarium, Laser Shows, and Butterfly Garden are extra.
Family memberships start at $70.

A First stop for small kids (up to eight years): the Discovery Center. Exhibits range from dinosaur bone replicas to real, live guinea pigs. Kids are free to roam around and learn a little more about science and the natural world as they move from one station to the next. Tots can stay put at the arts activity center, splash around at the water table, climb all over the place, and play with the best building blocks parents have ever seen—they're made of foam! One section of the Discovery Center is designated as an infant-only area. Toddlers on up will enjoy the other parts of the museum as well. The Butterfly Garden is always a huge hit, and if your child needs to burn off a little extra energy, trot over to the Science in the Park exhibit. Make sure to hit the Theater of Electricity and don't forget to check out a live animal presentation as well!

New England Aquarium

Central Wharf, Boston
617-973-5200 | www.neaq.org
Monday–Friday, 9AM–5PM; Saturday–Sunday until 6PM.
Adults, $19.95; children 3–11, $11.95; under 3, free.
Family memberships start at $100.

A We always find the aquarium a soothing, mysterious place. We talk a little more softly in here, wander the darkened halls, and stare, awe-stricken at the beautiful creatures behind illuminated tanks. Our all-time favorite is the aquarium's centerpiece: the giant ocean tank. The 200,000-gallon tank, formally named the Caribbean Coral Reef Exhibit, is a twenty-four-foot-deep reef filled with caves, sharks, turtles, and hundreds of tropical fish. A winding ramp leads up around the tank, and visitors can peek in windows as they stroll up four stories to the top.

Smaller children will love the tide pool exhibit where they can get wet and hold starfish.

Special activities such as playing with sea lions are available for an additional cost, but watching the penguins for hours is included in the price of admission. On the first and third Monday of every month, the aquarium hosts Aqua Kids Family Days. Stories, art, and live animal presentations are specifically geared toward young children in the Curious George Discovery Center. See chapter 2 for more information about the aquarium's Family Explorer classes for toddlers and preschoolers. Also, the aquarium offers whale watches and harbor tours right in Boston's own backyard—the Atlantic Ocean!

Old South Meeting House

310 Washington Street, Boston
617-482-6439 | www.oldsouthmeetinghouse.org
April-October, daily, 9:30AM–5PM; November–March, daily, 10AM–4PM.
Adults, $5; children under 18, $1.

P This is where it all began. At least, this is where the famous Boston Tea Party began. In 1773, five thousand colonialists, angry over taxes and the Boston Massacre, raced out of the meeting hall down to the harbor and dumped three shiploads of tea into the water. Of course, it took a couple more years and a few acts of defiance before the British attempted to put those upstart colonialists in their place. (*Psst ...* They didn't succeed!)

The Meeting House was built in 1729 and was the largest building in Boston at the time. A state-of-the-art audio tour will transport you and your little one back in time. You can ask for a family scavenger hunt kit that is geared toward your child's age. Or request the Anna's World Activity Kit, which is filled with hands-on objects and activities that explore the eighteenth century meeting house through the eyes of twelve-year-old congregation member Anna Green Winslow. If that doesn't strike your fancy, come by for a reenactment of the famous debates. Check the website for these special programs, which usually coincide with holidays and school breaks.

Old State House

Corner of State and Washington streets, Boston
617-720-3290 | www.bostonhistory.org
Daily, 9AM–5PM; January, daily, 9AM–4PM; July–August, daily, 9AM–6PM.
Adults, $5; children 6–18, $1; under 6, free.

🅿 The Old State House is Boston's oldest public building. The 1713 building was, at first, home to the British government; later it was the first place the Declaration of Independence was read aloud in Massachusetts. Every Fourth of July, the Declaration is read from the same balcony. At one time there was a plan to move the Old State House to Chicago's World Fair. Of course, no self-respecting Bostonian was going to allow that to happen. In 1879, the Antiquarian Club was formed to stop it from happening. The club evolved into the Bostonian Society, which to this day maintains extensive collections documenting all periods of our city's history.

Have your kids look for the lion and the unicorn sculptures outside, which represented British royal authority. The cobblestone circle outside the building marks the Boston Massacre site. The Boston Massacre was the killing of five colonists by British soldiers on March 5, 1770. It was the culmination of civilian-military tensions that had been growing since royal troops first appeared in Massachusetts to enforce the heavy tax burden imposed by the Townshend Acts almost three years earlier.

The younger set will like the permanent exhibit, A Hands on History, which gives kids the chance to recreate the Old State House's walls with foam bricks, peek behind the doors of the building's façade, and meet Otis, the Old State House's resident mouse.

Paul Revere House

19 North Square, Boston
617-523-2338 | www.paulreverehouse.org
Mid-April–October, daily, 9:30AM–5:15PM; November–April 14, daily, 9:30AM–4:15PM; closed Monday, January–March.
Adults, $3; children 5–17, $1.

🅿 *Listen, my children, and you shall hear / Of the midnight ride of Paul Revere...* From 1770 through 1800, Paul Revere owned this house, now the oldest remaining building in the downtown area. It was built around 1680, and much of the original building is intact. Truthfully, just walking through the house is not very interesting to small kids, but if you schedule your visit to coincide with one of the many events held throughout the year at the museum, it's a different story. Programs about life in colonial Boston, held every Saturday, May through October, can really charm the little ones. You'd be surprised how fascinated children are by these events, where everything from cutting silhouettes to music of the day is presented. Occasionally actors portray Revere, his wife, his mother-in-law, and others and will answer questions about their roles during the Revolutionary War. Check the website for various events and programs.

Sports Museum of New England

On the fifth and sixth floors of the TD Garden
Causeway Street, Boston
617-624-1234 | www.sportsmuseum.org
Schedule depends on TD Garden events. Always call before going. Generally open daily, 11AM–5PM. Admission is granted on the hour until 3PM (last entry).
Adults, $6; children 6–17, $4; under 6, free. Buy your tickets at the TD Garden box office.

P This is an essential stop for the pint-sized sports fan in the family. Exhibits cover the gamut—and explore New England's historical highlights of everything boxing, hockey, football, basketball, soccer, and baseball. Pretend you're catching a fastball from Roger Clemens at one interactive exhibit, watch old footage of the Boston Garden (true fans still lament its demise, but you can sit in old Garden seats at least!), and learn about local high school and college teams. Don't miss the Boston Bruins Hall of Fame portraits or the exhibit on the Boston Marathon.

USS Constitution and Museum

Charlestown Navy Yard, Boston
617-426-1812 | www.ussconstitutionmuseum.org
USS Constitution: April–October, Tuesday–Sunday, 10AM–5:50PM (last tour departs 4:30PM); November–March, Thursday–Sunday, 10AM–3:50PM (last tour departs 3:30PM). Tours available every half hour from 10:30AM.
Museum: April 15–November, 9AM–6PM;
November–April 14, 10AM–5PM.
Admission by donation.

P Old Ironsides, as the oldest commissioned warship afloat is affectionately called, makes its home at the Charlestown Navy Yard. If you ever get a chance to see the ship out in the harbor on the Fourth of July, it's a sight you and your kids will never forget. Crewmembers give daily

Deals & Free Admission Days

African Meeting House/Museum of African-American History
46 Joy Street, Boston
617-725-0022 | www.afroammuseum.org
Monday-Saturday, 10AM-4PM
Free

Boston Children's Museum
300 Congress Street, Boston
617-426-8855 | www.bostonkids.org
Friday nights are Family Dollar Night.
Admission is $1 per person from 5PM–9PM

Boston Fire Museum
344 Congress Street, Boston
617-482-1344 | www.bostonfiremuseum.com
May-November, Saturday, 11AM-4PM
Free

Franklin Park Zoo
1 Franklin Park Road, Boston
617-541-5466 | www.zoonewengland.com
Half-price the first Saturday of the month between 10AM and noon

Harvard Museum of Natural History
26 Oxford Street, Cambridge
617-495-3045 | www.hmnh.harvard.edu
Free to Massachusetts residents September–May,
Wednesday, 3PM–5PM; Sunday, 9AM–noon

Institute of Contemporary Art

100 Northern Avenue, Boston
617-478-3100 | www.icaboston.org

Free for children under age seventeen.
Free for adults, Thursday, 5PM–9PM

Free for families (up to two adults
accompanied by children twelve and under)
on the last Saturday of each month

MIT Museum

265 Massachusetts Avenue, Cambridge
617-253-5927 | www.web.mit.edu/museum

Free, Sunday, 10AM–noon

Museum of Fine Arts

465 Huntington Avenue, Boston
617-267-9300 | www.mfa.org

Kids are always free.
After 4PM on Wednesday, admission by donation

USS Constitution and Museum

Charlestown Navy Yard
617-426-1812 | www.ussconstitutionmuseum.org

Admission by donation

tours of the vessel every half-hour. The ship was built in 1797 and is most renowned for fighting off five British ships in the War of 1812. After the tour, visit the nearby museum for exhibits, hands-on activities, and artifacts detailing the long history of the warship.

No visit is complete without a walk around the Navy Yard. Now part of the park system, the Charlestown Navy Yard was one of the first shipyards built in the United States and remained a thriving shipyard for 174 years. Prior to that, the British landed here before the Battle of Bunker Hill. You can visit the nearby Bunker Hill Monument (55 Constitution Road, 617-242-5641; open daily, 9am–4:30pm) and climb up the 221-foot-high monument (294 steps) to get great views of the city, but make sure your kids can handle it, or you'll be stuck carrying them! Go to the Bunker Hill Pavilion to learn more about the battle in *Whites of Their Eyes*, a film named after the legend that the colonists weren't supposed to fire until they saw the whites of the Redcoats' eyes.

Live Theater

Boston Children's Theatre
Studios: 321 Columbus Avenue, Boston, MA
Performances: 186 Tremont Street, Boston, MA
617-424-6634 | www.bostonchildrenstheatre.org

P "Live Theater for Children by Children" is the motto of the Boston Children's Theatre, a seventy-five-year-old institution. Students in grades four to twelve perform productions such as *Annie, The Wizard of Oz*, and *The House at Pooh Corner*. Performances are geared to ages four and up. Most children are natural performers and getting a chance to watch their peers in action often fascinates them. In the summer, performances are held every Friday on George's Island, part of the Boston Harbor Islands national park area, which combines two great urban adventures: island hopping and theater going! Details on classes can be found in chapter 2.

Once Upon a Time with Kidstock
The Lyric Stage
140 Clarendon Street, Boston
617-437-7172 | www.lyricstage.com/kidstock

T On various weekends throughout the year, Once Upon a Time with Kidstock puts on interactive shows at The Lyric Stage. This is absolutely one of the best introductions to theater a kid can get. It's usually a raucous affair, with the children in the audience outnumbering the adults. Shows, such as *Jack and Jill and the Beanstalk*, always have a goofy twist, and several children from the audience are usually picked to perform with the adult actors. Everyone—and I mean everyone—has a great time.

Riverside Theatre Works
45 Fairmount Avenue, Hyde Park
617-361-7024 | www.riversidetheatreworks.org

P The non-profit Riverside Theatre Works puts on several family-friendly shows a year in an intimate venue in Hyde Park and uses lots of local kids in the productions. Recent performances include *Miracle on 34th Street, Hansel and Gretel,* and *Willy Wonka.* My daughter has attended their summer theater camp, a great program where the kids put on a show in three weeks! Details on classes can be found in chapter 2.

Wheelock Family Theatre
180 The Riverway, Boston (Wheelock College)
617-734-4760 | www.wheelock.edu/wft
Three mainstage productions annually.

P Wheelock Family Theatre focuses on shows that everyone can enjoy. Past productions include *Seussical* and *Charlotte's Web*. The theater works hard to attract all ages and annually offers one drama for adults, a musical, and a show for both children and adults. Classes for kindergarteners on up include dance, beginning Shakespeare, puppetry and drama, and much more. Visit the website to see what is on offer during any given semester.

Music

Boston Lyric Opera
Various locations
617-542-4912 | www.blo.org

P The Boston Lyric Opera always does at least one Family Day at the Opera every year (the 2009 show was *The Magic Flute*). Shows are staged in an hour and sung in English so the smallest kids will enjoy it. Performances are held at several locations around town. Afterwards the performers speak with the children about the production. Even adults wary of the opera should give this a chance! Visit the BLO website for details on venues and times, as well as interactive activities and articles to help you prepare for the performance.

Boston Symphony Orchestra/Boston Pops Orchestra

Symphony Hall
301 Massachusetts Avenue, Boston
617-266-1492 | www.bso.org
Family and youth concerts.

P The Boston Symphony Youth and Family Concerts are a fabulous introduction to the symphony for children. These concerts are also a bargain for music-loving parents, with much lower ticket prices than regular performances. After the show, tours of Symphony Hall are given, and pre- and post-concert activities include instrument demonstrations.

Barely Beyond Boston: Other Great Museums & Attractions

LIBRARIES

Brookline Public Library

361 Washington Street, Brookline
617-730-2370 | www.brooklinelibrary.org

A The main branch, built in 1869 (then replaced in 1910), sits in Brookline Village and has served as an important town icon for its almost 150-year history. The library established a separate children's reading room in 1890, an enormous step for the future of library services offered to children across the country. Today, each of the Brookline branches has numerous programs for kids (see chapter 5 for branch info). At the main branch, separate story times are offered for tots two years of age and for those three to five years of age; movies for preschoolers are offered every Friday morning at 10:30am. Other special programs are offered periodically throughout the year.

Cambridge Public Library

Longfellow School
359 Broadway, Cambridge
617-349-4030 | www.ci.cambridge.ma.us/~cpl

A Cambridge's main library consists of two buildings, one of which, the Van Brunt and Howe Richardsonian Romanesque building built between 1889 and 1902, is included in the National Register of Historic Places.

Families can find an impressive amount of special programming practically every day of the week, from toddler sing-a-longs to preschool story times to game nights. See chapter 5 for what the other branches have to offer.

See chapter 5 for what the other branches have to offer.

Newton Free Library
330 Homer Street, Newton Center
617-796-1360 | www.newtonfreelibrary.net

A Drop-in story times according to age, Pajama Story Times, preschool sing-a-longs, Science Tuesdays, music, Lego Club, and much, much more ensure there is something for every age at the library, located right in Newton Center. In 2008, the library became Newton's one and only, as the branches were closed due to budget cuts. Fortunately, the three-story library has plenty to offer the community.

MUSEUMS

Harvard Museum of Natural History
26 Oxford Street, Cambridge
617-495-3045 | www.hmnh.harvard.edu
Daily, 9AM–5PM.
Adults, $9; children 3–18, $6; under 3, free.
Free to Massachusetts residents September–May,
Wednesday, 3PM–5PM; Sunday, 9AM–noon.

P This is one of Boston's hidden treasures. I don't know many locals who've been here, which is too bad because they are missing out on a unique museum. Located in one rather sprawling structure, the Harvard Museum of Natural History shares the building with the Botanical Museum, the Museum of Comparative Zoology, and the Mineralogical and Geological Museum (admission covers all, plus the Peabody Museum of Archaeology and Ethnology—not always a big kid hit, so it's safe to skip it).

Sheer numbers are what you get here: 3,000 glass flowers, a 1,642-pound amethyst, a 42-foot-long prehistoric marine reptile, and so on. The vast amount of taxidermic animals (we call them statues for our young animal

Top 10 Family Adventures in Boston

Deirdre Wilson, senior editor of the *Boston Parents Paper*, a monthly magazine serving Eastern Massachusetts, and author of *The Lobster Kids' Guide to Exploring Boston* (Lobster Press, 2001), shares these Beantown family adventures:

1. **Make Way for Ducklings** sculptures at Boston's Public Garden, where author Robert McCloskey's book of the same name comes to life. Kids love to sit on the backs of the Mallard family depicted in the book.

2. A **Boston Duck Tour** on a World War II amphibious landing vehicle is good for sightseeing, Boston trivia, and plenty of laughs. Eventually, these vehicles splash into the Charles River for waterside views of Boston—and sometimes child passengers are chosen to man the steering wheel for a while.

3. In early June, head to City Hall Plaza for the annual **Scooper Bowl** where you can sample ice cream from top manufacturers—all for one small fee that benefits the Jimmy Fund.

4. **Faneuil Hall** is my children's hands-down favorite place to visit in Boston. We love to watch street performers, grab a slice of pizza, and sit outside for some fantastic people watching.

5. The **Museum of Science** is probably the number one choice for area families. My kids' favorite exhibits include the star shows at the Planetarium and the lightning demonstrations in the Theater of Electricity.

6. The **Boston Children's Museum** offers hours of fun for the young (and young at heart). Try the netted, tubular climbing structure, the Construction Zone, and the amazing Kid Power exhibits.

7. Gaze into seals and sea lions' deep brown eyes from the decks of the open-air exhibit space at the **New England Aquarium**.

8. At the **Franklin Park Zoo**, my girls adore the gorilla exhibit because the huge floor-to-ceiling display windows allow you to get up close and personal with the hairy beasts.

9. The **Skywalk Observatory** on the 50th floor of the Prudential Center offers 360-degree views of the city and beyond. Take the audio tour to see and learn about key historic and cultural sites in the city.

10. Tour the **USS *Constitution*** with U.S. Navy sailors, where you can stand at the huge steering wheel, run your hands over the cannons, and explore the officers' quarters below deck. Across the street at the museum, kids love operating the steering wheel, hoisting sails, and firing cannons.

lover) is unbelievable. It seems that the energetic Harvard ancestors caught one of every creature in the world for display here. After a field trip with my daughter's class, I was volunteered to take a bunch of kids back on a Saturday. Apparently, they loved it so much they felt a need for more time there!

MIT Museum

265 Massachusetts Avenue, Cambridge
617-253-4444 | www.web.mit.edu/museum
Daily, 10AM–5PM.
Adults, $7.50; children, $3; under age 5, free.
Sunday, free from 10AM–noon.

P The Massachusetts Institute of Technology's museum has the world's largest collection of holography. If your kids have ever gotten a hologram card in a cereal box and thought it was cool, wait until they see these! Holograms are really the tip of the iceberg at this interactive museum, which has all sorts of cutting-edge technology displays. Hands-on is the order of the day here. Kids can check out what MIT students and professors are up to in the Innovation Gallery, with rotating installations of recent inventions. And no one can fail to be fascinated by the Robots and Beyond exhibit, where you can see Kismet, the world's first sociable robot. The museum offers family programs throughout the year, such as the Cambridge Science Festival in the spring, and special school vacation activities. Check their website for event details.

Museum of Transportation

Larz Anderson Park
15 Newton Street, Brookline
617-522-6547 | www.mot.org
Tuesday–Sunday, 10AM–4PM.
Adults, $10; children 6–18, $5; under 6, free.
Family memberships start at $50.

P The centerpiece of Brookline's Larz Anderson Park (see chapter 6 for more on the park) is the Museum of Transportation, which opened in 1949. The museum contains "America's oldest car collection," assembled by Isabel and Larz Anderson, housed in the original carriage house, which was built in 1888 and is on the National Register of Historical Places. While the rotating exhibits upstairs are strictly off-limits to little fingers, the downstairs is devoted exclusively to tiny car lovers and (other than a large collection of vintage and rare automobile toys) allows for interaction. There is a pedal kart ride-on carousel and the bridge of a Boston Trolley with bell, continuously running. Kids will also like the automobile-related *Little Rascals* episodes and coloring supplies on a crafts table. Through spring, summer, and fall there are also weekly Sunday lawn events, free with museum admission.

Newton History Museum
The Newton History Museum at the Jackson Homestead
527 Washington Street, Newton
617-796-1450 | www.ci.newton.ma.us/jackson

P The Jackson family homestead was a stop on the Underground Railroad, which may come as a surprise to some. (I personally don't remember reading about Newton in my history books.) In the Abolition Room, kids can discover how slaves escaped to freedom. In the History Gallery, find out more about the earliest habitation by Massachusetts Indians to the end of the nineteenth century. Rotating exhibits are offered throughout the year, as are children's programs, such as Saturday Game Days.

LIVE THEATER

Coolidge Corner Movie Theatre (Children's Programs)
290 Harvard Street, Brookline
617-734-2501 | www.coolidge.org
October–March, Saturday, 10:30AM.
Live shows are $8; movies, $3.

P The Coolidge, Boston's only remaining open Art Deco movie theater, which is also a non-profit, offers a nice change of pace from regular Saturday morning cartoons at home. Every Saturday a family variety show is offered—and it's not just movies. Magic, dance, puppets, and classic cartoons are all part of the mix. Another one of my family's favorite activities is to go to the occasional interactive family movies at the Coolidge. Similar in feel to going to the *Rocky Horror Picture Show*, movies such as *The Princess Bride* are awesome when everyone in the packed audience is quoting the movie, brandishing blow-up swords, and ringing bells (all provided by the theater).

Magic Ark Children's Series
Leventhal-Sidman Jewish Community Center
333 Nahanton Street, Newton
617-558-6522 | www.lsjcc.org
Admission is $9.

T The Magic Ark Children's Series, usually offered on Sundays, showcases family entertainers, touring acts, and local performers. Catch a popular singer, such as Steve Roslonek of *SteveSongs;* a book brought to life, such as *Nate the Great*; or jugglers and circus acts, among others. All shows are open to the community at large; you don't need to be a JCC member.

Puppet Showplace Theatre
32 Station Street, Brookline
617-731-6400 | www.puppetshowplace.org
Performances during the school year: Saturday and Sunday, 1PM and 3PM; preschool show, Thursday, 10:30AM.
Summer performances: Wednesday and Thursday, 10:30AM and 1PM.
Daily performances during school breaks.
Admission is $9 per person for Family Shows.

P The Puppet Showplace Theatre is a magical experience, but make sure your kids are up for it. Some smaller children are afraid of puppets (as was my daughter). Weekend shows are for kids five years of age and older. Special "Tot" shows on Thursdays are targeted for ages three to five years; the puppeteers introduce themselves and the stories are more familiar. The theater is small, with less than one hundred seats. No seat is bad, but make sure you get one by reserving well in advance. A recent lineup of shows included *Cinderella, Peter Rabbit*, and *Puss in Boots*. After the show, the puppeteers will often allow children a closer look at the puppets, and sometimes (for a fee) you can make your own.
   Note: Tickets sell out regularly, be sure to book in advance.

Regent Theatre
7 Medford Street, Arlington
781-646-4849 | www.regenttheatre.com
Adults, $10; children, $8.

T This former vaudeville house has just five hundred seats, making it a perfect venue for its Family Fun Saturday Shows at 10:30am. These popular one-hour shows have featured everyone from singer Ben Rudnick to Jenny the Juggler and many other kid-pleasing performers. The shows are not weekly, so check the website for current listings.

Note: Tickets sell out quickly, be sure to book immediately after a show is announced.

Turtle Lane Playhouse
283 Melrose Street, Newton
617-244-0169 | www.turtlelane.org
Ticket prices vary.

P With a motto of "Broadway in Your Backyard," the Turtle Lane Playhouse delivers on its promise of affordable musicals and puts on about five shows a year. The small theater, with just 180 seats, is great for children, who don't have to strain to see the stage. Some of the family-friendly shows in the past include *Annie, Scrooge the Musical,* and *The Sound of Music.*

Alphabet Soup: Best Spots to Dine Out with Kids

JUST BECAUSE YOU have a child or two doesn't mean you can't go out for a nice meal—and I don't mean McDonald's. In fact, the younger your children are, the easier it is to transport them and keep them entertained, fed, or asleep. Many babies love the soothing sounds of quiet conversation and, as they get older, the variety of people to watch.

In a family-friendly city like Boston, you can take your child out to eat just about anywhere. You're almost always guaranteed to find a highchair and—under most circumstances—you won't receive any unfriendly looks with your meal. Of course, that doesn't mean dining out with your child or children is always easy. Even the most courageous parents have to be prepared to flee the restaurant with their untouched entrées in a doggy bag.

You may be able to avoid a public meltdown if you plan ahead and bring a bag of activities for your child (books, crayons, coloring books, toys that don't beep or buzz). Also consider packing a small snack in case the meal takes a while. It's a thin, thin line between being a little hungry and mildly cranky to becoming famished and totally irrational. If you don't think your child is up to dining out in the evening, but the foodie inside you is craving a well-crafted meal, try brunch. There is something magical about this perfectly timed meal—which segues nicely into a midday nap—and even restaurants without a children's menu usually offer single eggs, bagels, and fruit plates.

Here's an alphabetical list, from Aura to Zaftigs, of great, and perhaps unlikely, places to try. They include many of our family favorites across a broad range of cuisines and settings, from casual to high end. My pick for some of the best children's menus goes to Legal Sea Foods and Wagamama; both of these restaurants offer wholesome meals that kids love. If you're looking for something a bit more entertaining, try the pajama brunch at Tremont 647 and the family nights at Aura.

No matter what, keep in mind that if children learn how to behave in a restaurant early on, there's no reason why they can't dine at any four-star establishment in town.

Aura

1 Seaport Lane, Seaport District
617-385-4300 | aurarestaurant.com

A few of the city's swankest spots know kids can appreciate good food. Aura at the Seaport Hotel has a large children's menu and a fantastic program for families on Friday nights. It turns into a family dining restaurant and kid paradise with toys and a relaxed attitude. The chef, who has a toddler, also hosts a monthly lunch class focusing on how to make healthy baby foods. This is the perfect double date for two families with kids.

Bella Luna

284 Amory Street, Jamaica Plain
617-524-3740 | www.milkywayjp.com

When your pizza comes on plastic plates that have been decorated by kids, you know that you're in a family-friendly spot. Good thing that Bella Luna's pies are great, as is the rest of the menu. Casual, but serious about good food, this popular JP spot is an easy choice for no-stress dining.

Clink

215 Charles Street, Beacon Hill
617-224-4004 | www.clinkrestaurant.com

Clink at the Liberty Hotel is an unlikely spot for a family night out, but don't scoff. Go early enough to avoid the crowds and let the kids marvel at the hotel's cool setting. Set in a former jailhouse, the restaurant features remnants of cells, complete with bars. The kid's menu offers pretzel bites, mac-and-cheese, and spaghetti and meatballs.

Doyle's Cafe

3484 Washington Street, Jamaica Plain
617-524-2345 | www.doyles-cafe.com

I can't even estimate how many times my friends and I, kids in tow, have sat in the back room of Doyle's eating pub fare, happy to be in a place where there is plenty of room to spread out. Doyle's is casual and

☆ Tips for Dining Out with Kids from Robin Abrahams

Robin Abrahams is the weekly "Miss Conduct" columnist for the *Boston Globe Magazine*, and author of the book *Miss Conduct's Mind over Manners*. Here's her advice:

If table manners aren't important at home, they won't be important at a restaurant. Rehearse and reinforce the skills at home before opening night at Upstairs on the Square.

Honor your child's biological needs. You can't expect a child to behave well if she's up two hours past her bedtime or is eating dinner at seven o'clock when her last snack was at two o'clock in the afternoon. Be aware, too, that kids are usually skeptical about new foods (this is universal and has evolutionary reasons). Expecting a child to eat escargot at nine in the evening is a recipe for disaster.

If he has a meltdown, be prepared to take your kid out of the restaurant, and get him some other food pronto. This is consistent discipline for your child and shows courtesy to other patrons. It's always good to have a plan B in mind when taking your child out.

Never, ever change a baby's diaper in a restaurant booth. (You wouldn't think I'd have to say that, but I've gotten letters about this!) Breastfeeding mothers complain that they shouldn't have to feed their babies in the bathroom, and they have a point. No one should have to eat in a bathroom—so don't turn a dining room into one.

Sell your kids on the idea of table manners—and all manners—by presenting them as a way to be cool and grown-up.

boisterous enough to absorb the sound of crying babies with no problem. The pub, open since 1885, has a large bar area where a sports game is invariably playing, but the back rooms are perfect for families. We discovered Wikki Stix here for the first time, and that is enough to keep kids entertained for an entire meal.

El Oriental de Cuba
416 Centre Street, Jamaica Plain
617-524-6464

This super-popular Cuban restaurant has all the standards you'd expect and want, and in my family, that means rice, beans, and plantains for my young vegetarian. The atmosphere is very casual and can be a tiny bit hectic, but it always feels welcoming. Certainly there are always plenty of kids around. There can be a wait at times, so be prepared.

Full Moon
344 Huron Avenue, Cambridge
617-354-6699 | www.fullmoonrestaurant.com

Hands down, this is one of the best restaurants on either side of the river for families, especially those with babies or toddlers. The cheerful bustling spot has wonderful bistro food with a playspace in the back, proving that family-friendly and dining out are not mutually exclusive. Kids can opt for homemade mac-and-cheese or other tot favorites, all of which come with fruit and carrot sticks, while their parents can enjoy sophisticated dishes, such as Moroccan chicken or penne puttanesca. Invariably, kids finish their food first, but adults can eat at their leisure

One way to introduce your children to finer dining without a big price tag is to take them out during Boston's two restaurant weeks. In the winter and the fall, hundreds of restaurants try to drum up business during traditionally slow weeks. The prices are usually tied to the year, so in 2009, three-course pre-fixe menus were $20.09 for lunch and $30.09 for dinner. Make your reservations early. Visit www.bostonusa.com for more information.

because a train table, dollhouse, blackboard, and a plethora of toys engage the kids happily. The play area is within sight of almost all the tables, so you don't have to get up from your meal. Granted, no one would ever say this is a quiet restaurant, but that's a small price to pay for a lovely meal out.

Geoffrey's Café
4257 Washington Street, Roslindale
617-325-1000 | www.geoffreyscafebar.com

With a menu of comfort food galore, I challenge even the pickiest eater to have a problem finding something to eat. My daughter loves the gnocchi (bought from the neighboring Italian market) and the homemade mozzarella sticks, while my husband gravitates to the maple-glazed pork chop. If it's nice outside, we sit on the cozy patio.

Henrietta's Table
1 Bennett Street, Cambridge
617-661-5005 | www.henriettastable.com

Located at the Charles Hotel, Henrietta's Table is not just any hotel restaurant. The excellent food served here is usually fresh from a farm near you. There is a huge local following, and the all-you-can-eat Sunday brunch is legendary. The restaurant is casual and lively, so kids fit right in.

India Quality
484 Commonwealth Avenue, Kenmore Square
617-267-4499 | www.indiaquality.com

I adore Indian food and am just waiting for my daughter's palate to catch up and realize what it's missing. In the meantime, she can eat jasmine rice, garlic nan, and lentil soup while my husband and I stuff ourselves on saag paneer, tikka masala, and other delights. This spot offers some of the best in the city. My daughter does love all the aromas of Indian food, so I hope tasting will follow!

Johnny's Luncheonette

30 Langley Road, Newton Centre
617-527-3223 | www.johnnysluncheonette.com

Any place that serves breakfast all day is a no-brainer for families. Even if they won't eat anything else, you know pancakes or waffles are pretty irresistible to kids. Fortunately, Johnny's serves up plenty of other delicious diner dishes in a retro setting. Prices are unbelievable ($6.50 for a burger), and I think it's one of the only places around to get an egg cream. On the weekends, the line is out the door all day, so plan accordingly.

Kelly's Diner

674 Broadway, Somerville
617-623-8102 | www.kellysdiner.net

Visiting this 1953 diner is like time traveling. It's got the requisite Formica counters, complete with pies on top, plus an awesome breakfast menu. Kids love to play with the tabletop jukeboxes (which don't work) while they wait for their food. This is another spot where waits can be brutal, so go early or during off times if you can.

Legal Sea Foods

26 Park Plaza, Back Bay
617-426-4444 | www.legalseafoods.com (Search for other locations on website)

Parents magazine named Legal Sea Foods its number one family restaurant, and who am I to argue? The popular seafood restaurant has an extensive kid's menu that ranges from lobster to grilled cheese to fish-shaped ravioli. All the dishes come with fresh fruit and veggies.

Maggiano's Little Italy

4 Columbus Avenue, Theatre District
617-542-3456 | www.maggianos.com

Yes, okay, this is another chain, but it is the only one in Boston. Anyway, the giant portions are great for sharing. If your family consists of more than four members, you can choose a set menu that offers several options, and the food keeps coming until everyone is full! It's a busy spot for lunch and dinner, so there's no need to shush your kids.

No Name
15 Fish Pier, Seaport District
617-338-7539

If you really feel your little ones are just not up to eating someplace where they can't talk loudly or run around, this might be the spot for you. No Name is no nonsense, with bench seating and a very casual atmosphere. It's a love-it or hate-it place. I think the chowder is great, the seafood is always fresh, and if tablecloth dining is not in the cards, this is a perfect choice.

Olé Mexican Grill
11 Springfield Street, Cambridge
617-492-4495 | www.olegrill.com

Mexican is always a popular choice for my family. Cheese quesadillas are a staple dinner for my daughter, but when we go out, my husband and I like to try other dishes. Olé is known for its tableside guacamole appetizer, which is a must. You can also get salsa made to order just the way you like it. Any time a server prepares food by your table, your kids will be enthralled.

Petit Robert Bistro
Kenmore Square: 468 Commonwealth Avenue | 617-375-0699
South End: 480 Columbus Avenue | 617-867-0600
www.petitrobertbistro.com

Somehow a hot dog for dinner seems much more reasonable if it's a hot dog baguette with frites. At first glance, a French bistro might not seem particularly kid-friendly, but Petit Robert Bistro is a great spot to eat with your family. Adults can enjoy sophisticated creations, such as frog's legs Provençale (sure to freak your little ones out—or create some giggles) or braised lamb shank, while a full kid's menu ranges from pasta to a petit steak frites dish. Prices are very reasonable, and the lively atmosphere means no one looks at you when your toddler laughs a little too loudly. For a special treat, save room for the signature chocolate Eiffel Tower.

Faneuil Hall Marketplace, Boston
www.faneuilhallmarketplace.com

Locals will probably give me grief for this pick—after all, Faneuil Hall and the marketplace are for tourists, right? Well, with the dozens of eateries in the colonnade, everyone in the family can get something they like, from pizza to gyros to chowder. Most of the places offer samples, and the people-watching can't be beat.

Redbones

55 Chester Street, Somerville
617-628-2200 | www.redbones.com

Anywhere that you're encouraged to eat with your hands is a plus for families. When the food is as delicious as Redbones barbecue, it's also a win-win situation. This fun and funky spot, with upstairs and downstairs dining rooms, is decorated with posters of musicians and colorful murals. The $4.95 kid's menu, with catfish fingers, ribs, chicken fingers, and

---

Cooking Classes for Kids

There's no better way to engage kids in what they're eating than if they have a hand in creating it. They become more daring when they can see the process and can experiment.

Cooking to Learn
617-275-3014 | www.cookingtolearn.com
You can sign your little chef up for series of classes or just a one-time workshop with Cooking to Learn. Kids as young as three can get in the kitchen and get some hands-on kitchen skills. In the Cooks-n-Books series, the class creates one tasty treat inspired by a favorite children's book and then listens to a story as their dish cooks.

Create a Cook
53 Winchester Street, Newton
617-795-2223 | www.createacook.com
Create a Cook offers classes throughout the school year, plus holiday and summer camps, as well as one-off workshops for kids as young as three. Kids can learn with tools and workspaces scaled to their size. A great way to bond with your children is to take a parent/child workshop. How could you fail to have fun baking up chocolate treats?

pulled pork, includes a drink and is a bargain. If you can, ride your bike here, as your kids will no doubt get a kick out of the free bike valet service.

Sophia's Grotto
22R Birch Street, Roslindale
617-323-4595 | www.sophiasgrotto.com

My favorite neighborhood restaurant also happens to be my daughter's. She loves the Napoli pizza; I love any of the pasta dishes. This is a cozy little Mediterranean bistro in the heart of Rozzie Square. It is truly a place where everybody knows your name. There are so many regulars here that sometimes the place feels like a dinner party at someone's house. In the summer, tables in the outdoor courtyard are perfect for families. Kids can run around a bit, and twinkling lights make it magical in the dark. In colder weather, we make a beeline for the corner booth next to the kitchen to warm us up.

Tremont 647
647 Tremont Street, South End
617-266-4600 | www.tremont647.com

Going out for brunch in your pajamas? In public? Yes, you can. Tremont 647's long-standing pajama brunch is a blast, and your kids will love it. The servers outdo themselves in their choices of PJs, and the food is delicious. Homemade pop tarts, cinnamon French toast, and classic egg dishes are crowd pleasers.

Upstairs on the Square
91 Winthrop Street, Harvard Square
617-864-1933 | www.upstairsonthesquare.com

My daughter was forever impressed with Upstairs when we came for dinner and her Shirley Temple came with a Twizzler in it. That pretty much encapsulates the spirit of Upstairs. While the upstairs dining room might not be the best place for kids, the Monday Club room, decorated with eye-popping patterns and colors, has enough to distract even the busiest kid. There's always pizza on the menu (though you'll probably want to modify the toppings) and other kid-friendly items, such as burgers or grilled cheese sandwiches. Afternoon tea on Saturdays is excellent—and it'll prepare your kids for their first high tea at Harrods or the Ritz in London!

Villa Francesca
150 Richmond Street, North End
617-367-2948 | www.ristorantevillafrancesca.com

This is a classic in the North End, with brick walls, white table cloths, and usually a crowd, since it's close to the Freedom Trail. However, the food is wonderful, and no one looks twice if you come in with kids. At least in my family, Italian food has always been a family staple so finding something kid-friendly is a snap.

Wagamama
Boston: 1 Faneuil Hall Square | 617-742-9242
Boston: Prudential Center, 800 Boylston Street | 617-778-2344
Cambridge: 57 JFK Street, Harvard Square | 617-499-0930
www.wagamama.us

Besides just being plain fun to say, Wagamama offers what most kids can't resist: noodles. The Little Noodlers menu features a variety of ramen noodle dishes, with chicken, fish, or tofu. Die-hard chicken finger fans should like the chicken katsu, deep-fried chicken coated in panko. The casual, no-fuss restaurant is furnished with benches and tables, and they bring each meal as it is ready (instead of all at once), so hungry little ones won't be waiting long.

Yada Yada

34 Farnsworth Street, Seaport District
617-451-9232 | www.yadacafe.com

Next time you're at the Children's Museum around lunchtime, head to this family-owned spot around the corner that has perfect kid-friendly staple dishes. Grilled cheese and peanut butter and jelly sandwiches will please the tiniest guests, while a variety of sandwiches, plus some Albanian specialties, offers plenty of choices for adults. If you happen to be waiting for the museum to open, you can also get breakfast here at great prices.

Zaftigs Delicatessen

335 Harvard Street, Brookline
617-975-0075 | www.zaftigs.com

Another spot that serves all-day breakfast is a winner in my department, though I usually end up ordering potato pancakes and filling up too fast. This Jewish-style deli has an enormous menu, with everything from a bowl of borscht to BBQ brisket to a giant Reuben to smoked fish plates with fresh bagels. This is a very popular family restaurant, and the servers and the takeout counter are always hustling. On the weekends, the brunch line is out the door, so plan accordingly.

◆5 Baby, It's Cold Outside

AH... WINTER IN New England! Nothing is as beautiful as that first blanket of snow covering the ground, and who doesn't love to see a kid just *dying* to run outside, sled down a hill, and then charge up to do it all over again? The problem for parents and caretakers is the snow can lose its charm as the season wears on and on ... *and on.*

In this chapter, you'll find all the resources you need to make the best of this gorgeous and grueling season: refuges for when it's too cold to be outside and your four walls are closing in, outdoor activities that will have your toddler sleeping like a newborn again, and a handful of classes specific to the season.

First the refuges. Libraries, of course, are a cost-free lifesaver. With dozens of ongoing activities, story hours, and the like (and don't forget those free museum passes), you should plan on spending a good deal of time in your local branch. Bookstores also offer all sorts of free programs and craft hours. I certainly made the rounds when my daughter was tiny. Even when she was more interested in chewing on the books than reading them, it was a chance for me to interact with other moms. Eventually, you'll start to see the same faces and make some friends, and as your children get older, they will love these outings too.

For reasonable fees, you can also take your tot to an indoor playspace to while away a few hours. Many of Boston's community centers offer infant/toddler playtime hours, usually in the gyms, with soft toys and balls (see chapter 2 for information about classes). There are also several independently owned playspaces that may be worth checking out.

Parents of infants will love going to see a grown-up movie. Take advantage of the few places around town that offer baby-friendly afternoon matinees. It's a luxury that gets lost as they get older (alas, even if you do have great child care). Naturally, museums are wonderful in the winter, and this is where a membership really pays off. If you were so inclined, you could go to the Children's Museum every day of the week and participate in a new activity each day! (For more specific details on museums, check out chapter 3.)

Of course, just because it's winter, doesn't mean you have to hibernate. Greater Boston offers several indoor and outdoor ice rinks—many of which have skate rentals and lessons for children as young as two-and-a-half years—and a couple of decent sized ski hills for pee-wees. In fact, there are several Ski School programs for preschoolers on up. Finally, check out the nature preserves and their organizations for activities and additional ideas about how to make the most of our winter wonderland. The Department of Conservation and Recreation and Trustees of Reservations host regular activities such as Winter Walks for Families and Maple Sugar days, while the Massachusetts Audubon Society offers a range of programming for all ages, with family activities that make the most of the cold weather outside.

Indoor Playspaces

Blackstone Community Center

50 W. Brookline Street, Boston
617-635-5162
Tuesday and Thursday, 9:30AM–11AM.
Free.
Suggested membership is $10 per child per year; family of five membership for $75 per year.

T At this Boston community center, a toddler (ages two to five) playgroup is offered with toys and space to run around in the gym.

Boston Children's Museum Playspace

300 Congress Street, Boston
617-426-6500 | www.bostonkids.org
Daily, 10AM–4:30PM; Friday until 8:30PM.
Adults, $10; children 2–15, $8; age 1, $2; under 1, free.
Free for members.
Family memberships are available from $125; caregivers can be added for an additional $10. Membership includes admission to additional children's museums around the country.

I The Playspace is designed for infants up to age three. There's a tree house climber with bridges and slides, an extensive interactive toy train landscape, a messy area with a see-through painting wall, and an infant area with a waterbed and a soft space for crawlers. While you can drop in anytime, there are scheduled activities throughout the week; check the website to confirm days and times. Standard fare includes Messy Sensory Activities, which features Play-Doh, stamping, and water play; Music & Movement; Tasty Tuesdays, where kids can make nutritious snacks; and Story Time.

Curtis Hall Community Center

20 South Street, Jamaica Plain
617-635-5193
Tuesday, Thursday, and Friday, 10AM–noon.
$45 annual family membership required; $2 per child per session.

I Little ones can play with soft gym toys and balls, tumble on mats, or just run around. Many parents make this a routine stop during the winter, and loads of friendships—between both parents and their children—are made. The result is great neighborhood camaraderie.

Isis Maternity

Arlington: 397 Massachusetts Avenue
Boston: Prudential Center, 800 Boylston Street
Brookline: 2 Brookline Place
Needham: 110 Second Avenue
781-429-1500 | www.isismaternity.com

A Isis Maternity is one of the area's best parenting resources, offering classes, support groups, and retail in four locations in Boston and its surrounding neighborhoods. Purchasing a membership (which is a bargain) gives you great discounts on all of what Isis offers, but you don't have to join to enjoy their programs. For more information on Isis classes, see chapter 2, but Isis also offers drop-in playgroups, which are great resources whether your child is a newborn or a preschooler. Please check the Isis website for current schedules.

Open Play
Currently in Boston only.
Ages: Children must be mobile up to 3 years.
$10 for nonmembers; $7 for members.

Limit of ten kids. Open Play is held in a classroom, where you'll find a play kitchen, motor toys (steps and tunnels), puzzles, pull-toys, and more.

Playgroup Drop-In
All locations, one day per week; confirm schedule on the Isis website.
Ages: Up to 1 year.
$5 per family; free for members (including grandparents and caregivers).

Enjoy comfortable rooms with clean, age-appropriate toys.

Playgroup Drop-In
All locations, one day per week; check schedule on the Isis website
Ages: 1–3 years.
$5 per family; free for members (including grandparents and caregivers).

The drop-in groups are a great way to get your energetic toddler out of the house, tire them out with fun and games, and interact with new friends.

Kids Fun Stop
1580 VFW Parkway, West Roxbury
617-325-0800 | www.kidsfunstop.com
Monday–Thursday, 10AM–6PM; Friday until 5PM; Saturday–Sunday, 9AM–1:30PM.

$10 per two hours for one child; $16 for two kids; one adult per child, free.

A There are two large slides, plenty of climbing structures in different sizes, a playhouse, an arts and crafts area, Legos, blocks, and an enclosed infant play area. There's even a mini-carousel, which is a big hit with the kids, and an infinite number of riding toys and dress-up clothes. When your little one seems ready for a break, there's a cozy snack room available.

Nazzaro Community Center
30 North Bennet Street, North End
617-635-5166
Tuesday, Wednesday, and Friday, 9AM–noon.
$10 annual family membership.

I If you are a parent of an infant or a toddler up to age three, head to this gym so your kids can spread out and play. Similar to Curtis Hall, soft gym toys are provided.

Roslindale Community Center
6 Cummins Highway, Boston
617-635-5185 | www.roslindalecc.org
Tuesday–Friday, 9AM–10:30AM.
$50 family membership.

I The community center is home to a host of activities and programs. Visit the gym for newborns up to age four; the tots have space to run around, and you'll find plenty of toys for them to enjoy.

Barely Beyond Boston: Other Great Indoor Spaces

Beantown Playspace at Natick
Natick Collection
1245 Worcester Street, Natick
508-655-4800
Monday–Saturday, 10AM–9PM; Sunday, noon–6PM.

A A Boston-themed playspace decorated with the Green Monster from Fenway, the USS Constitution, and ducklings from the Public Garden. Definitely a great way to let the kids blow off steam when they're done with shopping (even if you aren't). Spoiler alert: You have to pass by Build-a-Bear Workshop and the Lego Store to get to the playspace!

Canton Totplex
5 Carver Circle, Canton
781-821-0304 | www.totplex.com
September–May, Monday–Friday, 9AM–2PM; closed all school breaks.
$8 per child; 10-day pass is $60.

A The Canton Totplex, located in the Canton SportsPlex, has an indoor playground on a turf soccer field, which is filled with climbers, slides, cars, and three moonwalks, one just for kids under age two. Little Tyke houses, saucers, and other backyard toys are plentiful. The space is divided according to age, and there is plenty of room to run around. A café on site offers lunch and snacks.

East End House Community Center

105 Spring Street, Cambridge
617-876-4444 | www.eastendhouse.org
Open every other Tuesday, 10AM–11:30AM.
Free.

A Every other week, a family playgroup is offered in the gym or the community room, with loads of toys, games, snacks, and a chance to socialize with other families. A facilitator is present to help engage both the kids and families.

ExploraZone at Mamas Move

45 Pond Street, Norwell
781-616-6244 | www.mamasmove.com
Monday–Thursday, 9:30AM–5PM; Friday, 9:30AM–4PM; Saturday, 9:30AM–3PM; Sunday, 10AM–2PM.
$7 for one child; each additional child is $5. Or opt for a $25 monthly fee for unlimited play. A one-time $25 enrollment fee is also required.

A This 5,000-square-foot facility is a dream for parents and kids. In the play area, there's a pre-walker area that is padded with soft climbing blocks and toddler toys. The older-kid area has play structures, a dress-up corner, a kids' tool shop, play café, reading corner, puzzles, trains, and blocks. There's also a café that offers snacks and coffee.

Imagination Island

12 Resnik Road, Plymouth
508-747-7447 | www.imaginationislandusa.com
Monday–Saturday, 10AM–5PM; Sunday, noon–5PM.
Monday–Friday, $9.50; Saturday–Sunday, $11.
Frequent Island Hopper pass is $96 and is good for twelve visits. Scheduled playgroups get a discount.

A There's a fourteen-foot-high climbing structure (enclosed), plus every little kid's favorite—a moon bounce. The space is large enough for kids to drive around in play cars, and there are Legos, doll houses, train sets, blocks, a play school house, fire truck, dress-up area, and much more. It's such a blast for the little ones that you'll have to drag your child out.

Kids Clubhouse

Atrium Mall
300 Boylston Street, Chestnut Hill
617-527-1400
Monday–Saturday, 10AM–9PM; Sunday, noon–6PM.
Free.

A The mall is often a great place to head in the winter. Shopping and food aplenty are available (with free parking as an added bonus). But as your baby gets older, their tolerance level will wane. The playspace at the Atrium Mall often bought me time to myself when my daughter wouldn't tolerate shops, especially if I went with a friend. If we had shopping to do, tag team babysitting the kids in the playspace was the ticket. The space has slides, cars, climbing structures, and other diversions. Additionally, the Atrium Mall houses a number of children's shops, some of which offer story hours and the like.

One Stop Fun

49 Power Road, Westford
978-692-9907 | www.onestopfun.com/gymmania.aspx
September–June, Monday–Thursday, 9AM–6PM;
Friday until 8PM; Saturday until 6PM; Sunday, 10AM–6PM.
Summer hours: Monday–Saturday, 9AM–4:30PM;
Sunday, 10AM–4:30PM.
Adults, free; ages 1 and up, $9.99.

A One Stop Fun has loads of classes and programs throughout the year, but the draw in winter is the indoor playground. There are three stories of tubes and tunnels to climb, a spiral slide, and a separate toddler area. A forty-foot traverse rock wall with a bouldering wall and a cave are really popular with the kids. A snack bar, with free wireless Internet, offers snacks and plenty of seating.

Independent Toy Stores

Frankly, big box toy stores overwhelm me. I'd much rather visit a store where the selections can be quirky and reflect the owner's personality. Plus, there's half a chance you'll find something that isn't totally ubiquitous. So when gearing up for the holidays, consider this list of great indie toy stores.

Boing! Toys

667 Centre Street, Jamaica Plain
617-522-7800 | www.boingtoys.com

Though small, there's a great selection of nifty toys and a great repeat customer program, which gives you discounts.

Green Planet Kids

22 Lincoln Street, Newton Highlands
617-332-7841

As the name suggests, this is an eco-friendly toy store packed with great products you won't find everywhere.

Hatched

5 Green Street, Jamaica Plain
617-524-5402 | www.hatchedboston.com

This is a small boutique that specializes in organic products from clothes to toys. The toy selection is small, but has unique offerings.

Henry Bear's Park

Arlington: 685 Massachusetts Avenue | 781-646-9400
Brookline: 19 Harvard Street | 617-264-2422
Cambridge: 361 Huron Avenue | 617-547-8424
www.henrybear.com

Around for more than thirty years, Henry Bear's Park stores have a huge and fantastic selection.

Kids R Kids

1952 Centre Street, West Roxbury
617-323-3991

This shop has a range of fun products, plus gifts, such as piggy banks and knick knacks that they can personalize with kids' names.

Kiwi Baby

1636 Washington Street, South End
617-247-2229 | www.kiwibabyboston.com
Two levels of the latest cool products and clothes. Easy to spend a lot of time here.

Magic Beans

Brookline: 312 Harvard Street | 617-264-2326
Cambridge: 361 Huron Avenue | 617-264-BEAN
Hingham: 94 Derby Street, Suite 255 | 781-749-2321
Wellesley: 200 Linden Street | 781-235-2120
www.mbeans.com

Huge selection of toys and gear, which the owners handpick. A bonus is that each of the three Magic Beans includes a Playscape, where the smallest customers can try out the store's wares. The downside? Trying to actually leave the store.

Stellabella Toys

Cambridge: 1360 Cambridge Street, Inman Square | 617-491-6290
Cambridge: 1967 Massachusetts Avenue, Porter Square | 617-864-6290
Burlington: Wayside Commons | 781-229-6290
Dedham: 950 Providence Highway, Dedham | 781-329-6290
www.stellabellatoys.com

Every Stellabella offers educational toys, plus lots of gear. Staff is super-friendly and always helpful.

Tadpole

37 & 58 Clarendon Street, South End
617-778-1788 | www.shoptadpole.com

This shop reflects its neighborhood, with artisan-inspired and contemporary products. Tadpole tries to blend the practical with the unique and whimsical items. Easily a Boston best.

Twinkle Star Baby Boutique

703 Broadway, Ball Square, Somerville
617-776-2340 | www.shoptwinklestar.com

This hip store offers environmentally friendly clothing, wooden toys, all sorts of gear, and there's a large play area for kids.

Wild Child

397 Massachusetts Avenue, Arlington
781-483-3566 | wildchildgear.com/store

Great selection of hand-picked products, from strollers to fashionable clothing, and of course, lots of interesting toys.

Retailers with Story Times & Activities

Below, you'll find listings for independent bookstores that host story hours. The major retailers, such as Borders and Barnes & Noble, have far too many stores to list here, but make sure to visit their websites to find their schedules. They almost always have something going on, and you could literally fill a week attending story hours at various locations.

Be on the lookout for other retailers—such as toy stores—that may also feature story times and activities. Pottery Barn Kids in the Atrium Mall at Chestnut Hill has been known to host a story time or two, as has the Natick Collection on Route 9. I've included a few of these retailers below, but this by no means represents the totality of what's on offer.

Barefoot Books

1771 Massachusetts Avenue, Cambridge
617-349-1610 | www.barefoot-books.com

A Barefoot Books publishes its own gorgeous books and sells them in their storefront. A story hour is offered on most Fridays and Saturdays, usually at 10:30am.

Blue Bunny

577 High Street, Dedham
781-493-6568 | www.dedhambluebunny.com

A The Blue Bunny is owned by author and illustrator of *The Dot,* Peter Reynolds, who also illustrates the Judy Moody book series. The book/toy store offers occasional story hours and special events.

Henry Bear's Park

Arlington: 685 Massachusetts Avenue | 781-646-9400
Brookline: 19 Harvard Street | 617-264-2422
Cambridge: 361 Huron Avenue | 617-547-8424
www.henrybear.com

A Some of the activities at Henry Bear's Park stores include a monthly family game night, new moms groups, character visits, and story times.

Magic Beans

Brookline: 312 Harvard Street | 617-264-2326
Cambridge: 361 Huron Avenue | 617-264-BEAN
Hingham: 94 Derby Street, Suite 255 | 781-749-2321
Wellesley: 200 Linden Street | 781-235-2120
www.mbeans.com

A Each of the three Magic Beans stores includes a Playscape, where the smallest customers can try out the store's wares. Convincing your child that they can't bring all those wonderful toys home can be a test of your fortitude. However, Magic Beans is truly magical. In addition, each location offers regular activities, such as story times, arts and crafts, and parent coffee hours. Check the individual store calendars on their website for details.

Porter Square Books

25 White Street, Cambridge
617-491-2220 | www.portersquarebooks.com

P A preschool story hour is offered every Wednesday at 11am. The children's section here is great too, and there are cozy cushions for kids to relax on.

Stellabella Toys

Burlington: Wayside Commons | 781-229-6290
Cambridge: 1360 Cambridge Street, Inman Square | 617-491-6290
Cambridge: 1967 Massachusetts Avenue, Porter Square | 617-864-6290
Dedham: 950 Providence Highway | 781-329-6290
www.stellabellatoys.com

A Every Stellabella, besides having a great selection of toys, offers myriad opportunities to gather with other parents. There are baby and toddler playgroups, sing-a-longs, new parent coffee hours, and some Music Together classes.

The Harvard Coop

1400 Massachusetts Avenue, Cambridge
617-499-2000 | www.harvardcoopbooks.bncollege.com

A On Tuesdays, usually at 11am, the Coop hosts a preschool story time. Saturdays, also around 11am, the Coop hosts a story time where kids under age seven are welcome. Cookies and juice are offered at both story times. Head to the children's section in the lower level for programs.

Movies

Baby Friendly Movies

Capitol Theatre
204 Massachusetts Avenue, Arlington
781-648-4340 | www.somervilletheatreonline.com/capitol
Monday afternoons.
Admission is $5.

i Capitol Theatre features a baby-friendly movie (new releases) every Monday afternoon, meaning parents with babies are welcome. The sound is kept low so it doesn't hurt little ears, and the lights are kept slightly high so you can see enough to nurse. All in all, an excellent and relaxing Monday afternoon activity.

Box Office Babies

Coolidge Corner Theatre
290 Harvard Street, Brookline
617-734-2500 | www.coolidge.org/babies
Alternate Fridays, 1PM.
Admission is $6.75.

i Bi-monthly, baby-friendly screenings of current features on the giant screen are offered every other Friday. Bathrooms have Koala changing tables, and there's room in the lobby to park strollers and stretch out.

Libraries

Every single branch of the Boston Public Library hosts story hours, puppet shows, sing-a-longs, and other special activities throughout the year. Visit the main website (www.bpl.org) for calendar listings and links to the offerings at specific branches. Also, don't forget to see what free or discounted museum passes the library offers. All you need in order to take advantage of this wonderful perk is a free library card. Keep in mind that there is no age requirement for library card holders, so as soon as your child shows an interest, let him get his own. Kids under twelve simply need their parents' permission, but that's it! My daughter got her very own card when she was two, and it was one of her proudest moments.

BOSTON

ADAMS STREET BRANCH: 690 Adams Street | 617-436-6900

BRIGHTON BRANCH: 40 Academy Hill Road | 617-782-6032

CENTRAL LIBRARY: 700 Boylston Street | 617-536-5400

CHARLESTOWN BRANCH: 179 Main Street | 617-242-1248

CODMAN SQUARE BRANCH: 690 Washington Street | 617-436-8214

CONNOLLY BRANCH: 433 Centre Street | 617-522-1960

DUDLEY BRANCH: 65 Warren Street | 617-442-6186

EAST BOSTON BRANCH: 276 Meridian Street | 617-569-0271

EGLESTON SQUARE: 2044 Columbus Avenue | 617-445-4340

FANEUIL BRANCH: 419 Faneuil Street | 617-782-6705

FIELDS CORNER BRANCH: 1520 Dorchester Avenue | 617-436-2155

GROVE HALL BRANCH: 41 Geneva Avenue | 617-427-3337

HONAN-ALLSTON BRANCH: 300 North Harvard Street | 617-787-6313

HYDE PARK BRANCH: 35 Harvard Avenue | 617-361-2524

JAMAICA PLAIN BRANCH: 12 Sedgwick Street | 617-524-2053

LOWER MILLS BRANCH: 27 Richmond Street | 617-298-7841

MATTAPAN BRANCH: 1350 Blue Hill Avenue | 617-298-9218

NORTH END BRANCH: 25 Parmenter Street | 617-227-8135

ORIENT HEIGHTS BRANCH: 18 Barnes Avenue | 617-567-2516

PARKER HILL BRANCH: 1497 Tremont Street | 617-427-3820

ROSLINDALE BRANCH: 4239 Washington Street | 617-323-2343

SOUTH BOSTON BRANCH: 646 East Broadway | 617-268-0180

SOUTH END BRANCH: 685 Tremont Street | 617-536-8241

UPHAMS CORNER BRANCH: 500 Columbia Road | 617-265-0139

WASHINGTON VILLAGE BRANCH: 1226 Columbia Road | 617-269-7239

WEST END BRANCH: 151 Cambridge Street | 617-523-3957

WEST ROXBURY BRANCH: 1961 Centre Street | 617-325-3147

Barely Beyond Boston: Additional Libraries

BROOKLINE

MAIN BRANCH: 361 Washington Street | 617-730-2370
www.brooklinelibrary.org

COOLIDGE CORNER: 31 Pleasant Street | 617-730-2380

PUTTERHAM: 959 West Roxbury Parkway, Chestnut Hill
617-730-2385

CAMBRIDGE

MAIN PUBLIC LIBRARY: Longfellow School, 359 Broadway
617-349-4030 | www.cambridgema.gov/CPL
BOUDREAU BRANCH: 245 Concord Avenue | 617-349-4017
CENTRAL SQUARE BRANCH: 45 Pearl Street | 617-349-4010
COLLINS BRANCH: 64 Aberdeen Avenue | 617-349-4021
O'CONNELL BRANCH: 48 Sixth Street | 617-349-4019
O'NEILL BRANCH: 70 Rindge Avenue | 617-349-4023
VALENTE BRANCH: 826 Cambridge Street | 617-349-4015

NEWTON

NEWTON FREE LIBRARY: 330 Homer Street, Newton Center
617-796-1360 | www.newtonfreelibrary.net

Outdoor Activities

Of course, once your children are old enough to enjoy a good snow fall, you might not want to spend every second of your day indoors. Here are a handful of activities that you can use to speed the season, while introducing your child to the joys of the outdoors!

ICE-SKATING

Bay State Blades
781-826-8798 | www.baystateblades.com

T This organization offers skating classes around Boston. They start young, offering lessons to children as young as two-and-a-half. Call or visit their website for more information.

Bay State Skating School
781-890-8480 | www.baystateskatingschool.org

P Bay State Skating School provides ice-skating lessons for children (ages 4.5 and up) at many of the DCR rinks. This is how my daughter learned to skate, and it was way more effective than her trying to learn from my husband (though his attempts were noble and appreciated). Keep in mind: they don't hold anyone's hand. They teach the kids how to fall and get up, and the kids learn very quickly.

Classes are for beginner, intermediate, and advanced students, with no more than ten students per class.

Charles Hotel
1 Bennett Street, Cambridge
617-864-1200 | www.charleshotel.com; Click: Service & Amenities
Generally open December–March, Monday–Friday, 4PM–8PM;
Saturday, Sunday, and holidays, 10AM–8PM.
Admission includes skate rental:
Adults, $5; under 12, $3; family of four, $10.

P This is a cute little winter rink set up on what is normally a patio area in front of the hotel. It's perfect for little kids, and the hotel even provides crates for beginners to lean on. Private lessons are available by appointment, and there is a small concession stand for when your tiny skater needs hot chocolate to warm up. The rink is also available for private events.

617-626-1250 | www.mass.gov/dcr; Search: Skating

A The DCR runs a number of rinks around the area. Public skating hours vary at each rink. I can't stress enough that you should call before you go. Often rinks are booked by skating clubs or hockey teams or closed due to weather or maintenance. Double checking will save you aggravation, and please don't rely on the website for accurate information. Call!

BAJKO MEMORIAL RINK
75 Turtle Pond Parkway, Hyde Park | 617-364-9188

DALY MEMORIAL RINK
Nonantum Road, Brighton | 617-527-1741

DEVINE MEMORIAL RINK
995 Morrissey Boulevard, Dorchester | 617-436-4356

EMMONS HORRIGAN O'NEILL MEMORIAL RINK
150 Rutherford Avenue, Charlestown | 617-242-9728

JIM ROCHE COMMUNITY ICE ARENA
1275 VFW Parkway, West Roxbury | 617-323-9512

KELLY OUTDOOR RINK
1 Marbury Terrace, Jamaica Plain | 617-727-7000

MURPHY MEMORIAL RINK
Day Boulevard, South Boston | 617-269-7060

PORAZZO MEMORIAL RINK
Constitution Beach, East Boston | 617-567-9571

REILLY MEMORIAL RINK
355 Chestnut Hill Avenue, Brighton (Cleveland Circle) |
617-277-7822

SIMONI MEMORIAL RINK
Gore Street, Cambridge | 617-354-9523

STERITI MEMORIAL RINK
561 Commercial Street, North End | 617-523-9327

VETERANS MEMORIAL RINK
570 Somerville Avenue, Somerville | 617-623-3523

Boston Common, Boston
617-635-2120 | www.bostoncommonfrogpond.org
Hours are weather-dependent.
November–March, Tuesday–Thursday and Sunday, 10AM–9PM;
Monday until 5PM; Friday–Saturday until 10PM.
Adults, $4; under 13, free.
Skate rental: Adults, $8; under 13, $5.
Consider a family season pass (in 2008–09, it was $150) if you
plan to skate a lot.

P Absolutely one of the most beautiful places I know of to skate outdoors, especially at night, when the lights of the city are your backdrop. It can get busy here, but it's still a magical place. The Frog Pond Skating School offers a variety of group lessons for children ages three and up, and private and semi-private lessons for skaters of all ages.

300 Athenaeum Street, Cambridge
617-492-0941 | www.paddleboston.com/skating2/skating.php
December–March, Tuesday–Thursday, noon–8PM;
Friday until 9PM; Saturday, 11AM–9PM; Sunday, 11AM–6PM;
Monday, noon–5PM (excluding holidays).
Adults, $4; under 10, $1.
Skate rental: $5.

P Managed by Charles River Recreation, this rink is right outside the MIT campus, so don't be surprised to see lots of students zipping around. Both group and private lessons are offered here.

23 Newton Street, Brookline
617-739-7518
www.townofbrooklinemass.com; Search: Ice Skating Rink
Generally open December–February, Tuesday and Thursday,
10AM–noon; Friday, 7:45PM–9:45PM; Saturday–Sunday, noon–5PM.
Call for admission prices (Brookline residents get a discount).

P This outdoor rink in the heart of Larz Anderson Park offers a fun spot for some ice time. The Bay State Skating School offers classes here too (see listing above). In addition, there are some fantastic hills to sled down if the rink is busy or closed.

SKIING, SNOWBOARDING, SNOWSHOEING & TUBING

Amesbury Sports Park

12 South Hunt Road, Amesbury
978-388-5788 | www.amesburysportspark.net
Thursday–Friday, 3:30PM–9PM; Saturday, 10AM–9PM; Sunday until 7PM.
Thursday, three-hour pass is $15; five-hour pass is $20. Friday–Sunday, three hour pass is $20; five-hour pass is $30.

P There are lots of lanes to slide down and three lifts to take you to the top. They make snow here, so it's not completely weather-dependent. Kids have to be older than four and accompanied by an adult. If they are less than forty-two inches tall, they also have to wear a helmet.

Blue Hills Reservation

Blue Hills Ski Area
4001 Washington Street, Canton
781-828-5070 | www.ski-bluehills.com
Sunday, 9AM–5PM; Monday–Wednesday, 2PM–9PM;
Thursday–Saturday, 9AM–9PM.
Prices vary with day, hours, and ages; call to check.

P The Blue Hills Reservation encompasses more than seven thousand acres from Quincy to Dedham, Milton to Randolph. There are any number of classes, camps, and private lessons available for kids as young as age four. Visit the website for the huge amount of options, including ski and snowboard packages.

Nashoba Valley Ski Area and Tubing

Littleton: 179 Great Road
Westford: 79 Powers Road
978-692-3033 | www.skinashoba.com
Monday–Friday, 9AM–10PM; Saturday–Sunday, 8:30AM–10PM.
Admission varies with days and hours; call for rates.

P Nashoba offers private lessons for kids age three and up and group lessons for age four and up. In addition to skiing, there's a nearby tubing park. You have to be age six and up or over forty-two inches to tube. There are fifteen lanes and four lifts.

Wachusett Mountain Ski Mountain

499 Mountain Road, Princeton
978-464-2300 | www.wachusett.com
Monday–Friday, 9AM–10PM; Saturday–Sunday, 8:30AM–10PM.
Admission varies with days and hours; call for rates.

P This is another great spot to get your kids up and running on skis or snowboards. Polar Kids classes are for little skiers and snowboarders ages four to twelve; each child is placed in age- and skill-appropriate groups. The Wachusett crew must know what they are doing: they teach more than ten thousand students per year!

Weston Ski Track

198 Park Road, Weston
781-891-6575 | www.skiboston.com/skitrack/skitrack.php
Call for hours and prices.

P This cross-country ski and snowshoeing center uses natural snow and grooms fifteen kilometers of trails. In addition, snowmaking on a two-kilometer lighted loop provides consistent snow conditions and reliable night skiing. Snowshoeing is also an option on the trails. There are a variety of classes on offer: Kinder Lessons (for ages four to five) are one hour, taught through fun and games, and limited to four students. Children six to ten are given more advanced instruction. Skiers and snowshoers eleven to twelve years of age can receive a discounted rate for adult lessons. Private lessons are also available. In addition, there is an Introduction to Snowshoeing that will get everyone in the family comfortable.

OTHER OUTDOOR ADVENTURES

Department of Conservation and Recreation

www.mass.gov/dcr

A The Department of Conservation and Recreation doesn't hibernate! In addition to overseeing all the public skating rinks in Massachusetts, the DCR sponsors a variety of programming to help your family explore the snowy side of nature.

Mass Audubon

www.massaudubon.org

A Mass Audubon offers an incredible range of programming throughout the year—including the winter. Many of the reservations in the Greater Boston area offer both drop-off and parent-participation events. Some fees apply, though you can find free events as well. Check out their website to see what's going on.

Trustees of Reservations

www.thetrustees.org

A Make sure to take a look at the website for the Trustees of Reservations to see what's doing during the winter. Generally, the Trustees offer snowshoe tours, walks to look for winter animals, and other fun activities to get the blood flowing!

6 It's Hot, Hot, Hot

BOSTON'S SCENE CHANGES dramatically in the summer. The city transitions into an entirely different place. College students go home, and a good number of locals flee to the Cape or their equivalent summer spots. It's as if the city takes a deep breath. There's more parking, less traffic, and fewer lines at your favorite haunts. Sure, the city may get a little busy with out-of-town vacationers, but popular tourist destinations are easily avoided—especially if you know your options.

What Boston offers the youngest set is a summer of exploring wonderful green, open spaces. In fact, there are so many parks and playgrounds in and around the city, it would be impossible to list them all here. And as every parent knows, convenience is key: nothing beats your own neighborhood park.

Sometimes though, a change of scenery is in order. What you'll find here are my picks of spots worth the trip. Choose among green spaces, parks, playgrounds, wading pools, spray decks, and a few beaches for good measure. Pack a picnic, plenty of sunscreen, and enjoy the sunny days while you can.

Beaches

Beaches in Boston? You bet! Believe it or not, they are clean, pleasant, and safe for swimming—with playgrounds and picnic tables nearby so you can make a day of it. Thanks to the hard work of local government and countless non-profits, even the most skeptical Boston native can dive into our waters. The few public beaches in Boston are managed by the Department of Conservation and Recreation (DCR) and are open from dawn to dusk. For information on any of them, call 617-727-5290 or visit www.mass.gov/dcr.

Constitution Beach
Orient Heights, East Boston

There's a bathhouse, large playground, picnic area, tennis and handball courts, shaded areas, and foot showers. Lifeguards are on duty during the summer. On the shoulder seasons, you can still swim, but it's at your own risk.

Dorchester Shores Reservation
Malibu Beach, Savin Hill Beach, and Tenean Beach
Morrissey Boulevard, Dorchester

A surprisingly underutilized section of Boston, this pathway and greenway system runs from Castle Island in South Boston all the way to the Neponset River. The wide promenade is a fantastic place to teach kids how to ride a bike or let them scooter around. You can swim at Malibu Beach, which offers lifeguards and a bathhouse; Savin Hill Beach, which also has a tot lot; and Tenean Beach, which has a playground, shaded areas, picnic tables, and a boardwalk.

Pleasure Bay, L and M Street Beaches, and Carson Beach
Day Boulevard, South Boston

A three-mile stretch of beaches and parks make up Dorchester Bay—a refreshing place to catch the ocean breeze on a hot and humid day in the city. Carson Beach has public restrooms and lifeguards. L and M Street Beaches are adjacent to each other and link the beach at Pleasure Bay with Carson Beach, providing one of the longest stretches of uninterrupted beach in the Boston area. The Edward J. McCormack Bathhouse at Carson Beach has restrooms, changing rooms, showers, drinking water fountains, chess tables, and bocce courts. Pleasure Bay is a calm, enclosed lagoon with a sandy beach for swimming. Foot showers and water fountains are a bonus. The bay is fully enclosed by the man-made Head Island Causeway, so the water quality is good.

Set Sail to the Boston Harbor Islands!

Believe it or not, there are over thirty islands in Boston Harbor, many of which are open to exploration. Ferries are easy to catch from the South Shore and Long Wharf, and they can transport you in no time at all to Spectacle Island (which has a public swimming beach), George's Island (home to Fort Warren, a Civil War fort), and to Peddocks Island (great for taking a nature walk). What few Bostonians realize, however, is that there is programming especially designed for children throughout the summer. From live music to Boston Children's Theatre performances to turn-of-the-century baseball games or building your own kite, the Harbor Islands offer the youngest residents of the Greater Boston area a chance to explore their local history and a little piece of wilderness right in their own backyard. If you're looking for a truly special trip to the islands, consider pitching a tent with your family and spending the night. For more information on all the available activities, visit www.harborislands.org.

Watery Delights: Spray Decks, Pools, and the Like

Something about sprinklers just calls to kids. These little folks could spend hours darting in and out of the jets, shrieking with delight when the water catches them. And since spray decks are almost always found next to playgrounds, kids will run themselves silly moving between the two, which is parent-speak for the makings of an excellent naptime. In this section you'll find some sprinkler parks that are worth a special trip, such as the Frog Pond in Boston Common or the Artesani on the Charles River.

Boston's city pools can get amazingly crowded and sometimes are so overrun with day campers, it's not even worth bothering to go. Nevertheless, when it's a hot day and swimming seems like the only option for surviving the heat, head to the pool early or late to avoid the crowds. And make sure you call ahead to check that it is open. I've shown up at pools only to find out that they are undergoing maintenance or are packed to capacity. There's nothing like promising your child a swim only to disappoint them and ruin everyone's day.

Like the beaches, most of Boston's other water attractions are managed by the DCR. Most spray pools are open from dawn to dusk. For information on any of them, call 617-727-5290 or visit www.mass.gov/dcr. DCR pools offer free admission.

Artesani Park and Wading Pool
1255 Soldiers Field Road, Brighton

This is one of the best spray parks in the city. Located on the Charles River, you get a wonderful view and a hugely popular wading pool. There are lifeguards on duty, showers, changing rooms, picnic tables, two playgrounds (one for toddlers and one for older kids), and free parking! Bring bread to feed the ducks if you decide to take a walk on the water's edge. And carry some cash for the ice cream truck that is pretty much parked in the lot all day. The water here is almost always freezing, so pack an extra T-shirt in case your kids need it.

Christian Science Plaza
175 Huntington Avenue, Boston
617-450-2000 | www.themotherchurch.org; Search: Plaza
Daily, dawn to dusk.

On the grounds of the massive Church of Christ property, you'll find a beautiful reflecting pool and an enormous fountain that delights local and visiting kids in the summer. It's so popular that camps make trips here in the afternoon to cool off their charges. There are shaded areas and plenty of places to plop down if you want to bring a picnic and make an afternoon of it (the Prudential

Center is conveniently located across the street for restrooms and any other last minute necessities).

Frog Pond Spray Pool & Fountain
Boston Common, Boston
617-635-2120 | www.bostoncommonfrogpond.org
June-Labor Day, daily, 10AM-6PM.

In July and August, the Common's Frog Pond becomes a six-inch deep wading pool with a spray head fountain in the middle. It is, as to be expected, extremely popular. If it gets too crowded, kids can take a break at the adjacent Tadpole playground, which holds a seven-week summer Celebrity Reading Series in connection with ReadBoston. Kids not only get entertained with a story, they get to take home a book! The event usually happens once a week on Thursdays in July and August. Check www.tadpoleplayground.org for details.

Swan Boats
Public Garden, Boston
617-522-1966 | www.swanboats.com
April-June 20, daily, 10AM-4PM; June 21-Labor Day, daily, 10AM-5PM;
Labor Day-September 20, Monday-Friday, noon-4PM;
Saturday-Sunday, 10AM-4PM.
Adults, $2.75; children 2-15, $1.50.

The 130-year-old Swan Boats have to be one of the most charming and iconic activities offered in the city. No tot fails to love them, especially if they've read *Make Way for Ducklings*—the official children's book of Massachusetts. After your fifteen-minute ride on these human-paddled boats, wander over to the Public Garden to find the statues inspired by the same book. One more way to celebrate the book is to attend the annual Duckling Day Parade on Mother's Day. Dressed as ducklings, kids and their families retrace the steps of Mrs. Mallard and her family of eight ducklings. The Harvard University Marching Band leads the way for this adorable event. The $25 fee to participate goes to the non-profit Friends of the Public Garden. Of course, watching is free. Visit www.friendsofthepublicgarden.org for more information.

ADDITIONAL WATERY DELIGHTS

Allston-Brighton Swimming and Wading Pool
380 North Beacon Street, Brighton

Lee Memorial Wading Pool
280 Charles Street, Boston

Mission Hill Spray Deck
Behind Boston Police Headquarters
Southwest Corridor Park, Roxbury

Moynihan Wading Pool
920 Truman Parkway, Hyde Park

Olsen Swimming and Wading Pool
95 Turtle Pond Parkway, Hyde Park

Reilly Memorial Swimming Pool
355 Chestnut Hill Avenue, Cleveland Circle, Brighton

Ryan Wading Pool
350 River Street, Mattapan

Stony Brook Spray Deck
Corner of Lamartine and Boylston streets
Southwest Corridor Park, Jamaica Plain

Sailing & Boating

Charles River Canoe & Kayak

1071 Soldier's Field Road, Allston-Brighton
617-462-2513 | www.paddleboston.com
May–October, Saturday, Sunday, and holidays, 10AM–7PM;
Friday, 1PM–7PM; June–August, Thursday, 1PM–7PM.
All rates listed are hourly: Standard canoe (two adults/two kids), $15; kayaks for adults, $14; double kayaks, $16; children's kayak (age 6–12), $7.

P Down the road from the Artesani Park (see Watery Delights section above), Charles River Canoe & Kayak offers a wonderful outing on the river—great for a spontaneous family activity. You can rent a rowboat, canoe, or kayak and meander down nine miles of the Charles River. Because there is no current, it's light work and hassle-free. All you have to do is show up, pick a boat, and you're off! My family enjoys kayaking, so with my husband and daughter in a double kayak and me in a single, we paddle back and forth and love seeing Boston's skyline from the water. The company also offers rentals in Newton and Natick (by appointment) and classes and camps for older children.

Jamaica Pond, Jamaica Plain
617-268-7243 | www.courageoussailing.org
April 1-Veteran's Day, daily, 10AM-6PM.
Rowboat, $10 an hour; sailboat, $15 an hour.
Boats may not be available when youth programs are going.

P Gather up the kids and row, row, row—or sail—your boat out on this giant kettle hole. You can't swim in the pond, as it is Boston's reserve water supply, but you can enjoy paddling around, fishing, and feeding the ducks and geese.

Playgrounds

There are literally hundreds of playgrounds in Boston, ranging from enormous ones on the Esplanade to more modest ones at nearby public elementary schools. It's amazing how taking your child to a new playground is such a treat. It's a brand-new place to discover, make new friends, and explore different structures. Here are my family's top five around the city.

Castle Island and Fort Independence

Day Boulevard, South Boston
617-727-5290

Fort Independence is a granite fort that was built between 1834 and 1851 on Castle Island, at the tip of Pleasure Bay. It's a fantastic spot for your curious future pilots and engineers to watch planes as they land and take off from Logan. On summer weekends you can take free tours of the fort, but really the main attraction here for kids is the space to bike, skate, or chill. Stop in at the local landmark Sullivan's for snacks if you get hungry (the hot dogs are great). Walk down to Carson Beach for a nice playground. You may see a theme emerging: if there's both a playground and a water view, everyone in the family is happy.

Christopher Columbus Park

Atlantic Avenue, North End

This playground, with its structure shaped like a ship, is located right on Commercial Wharf. It's perfect for the kids to pretend they are sailing off to sea. You can sit and watch the action in the harbor or wander over

Children's Indie Bookstores

I love nothing more than to hang out in a bookstore, and if it's locally owned by people that can take the time to talk to me or my daughter about their favorite books, all the better. Not all of these focus solely on kids, but they all have fantastic children's sections...and they are air conditioned!

Barefoot Books

1771 Massachusetts Avenue, Cambridge 617-349-1610 | www.barefoot-books.com
Barefoot Books publishes its own gorgeous books and sells them in their storefront.

Blue Bunny

577 High Street, Dedham
781-493-6568 | www.dedhambluebunny.com
The Blue Bunny is owned by the author and illustrator of *The Dot*, Peter Reynolds, who also illustrates the Judy Moody book series.

Brookline Booksmith

279 Harvard Street, Brookline
617-566-6660 | www.brooklinebooksmith.com
Maybe not the largest children's section in town, but a thoughtful one, with a great selection.

Children's Book Shop

237 Washington Street, Brookline
617-734-7323 | www.thechildrensbookshop.net
This long-established bookstore (open since 1977) has thousands of books in stock. One of the best things here though is the knowledgeable staff. No matter how vague the description your little bookworm provides—*bam!*—the staff will produce it.

Curious George & Friends

1 JFK Street, Cambridge 617-498-0062 | www.curiousg.com

Two floors of books and toys, and not all focused on the little monkey, even though the store was founded with help from *Curious George* author Margret Rey.

New England Mobile Book Fair

82-84 Needham Street, Newton Highlands 617-964-7440 | www.nebookfair.com

This enormous store is a great place to browse. With the thousands of books that seem to lack any organization, a quick stop here is unrealistic—but oh the treasures you will find!

Porter Square Books

25 White Street, Cambridge 617-491-2220 | www.portersquarebooks.com

The children's section here is huge, and there are cozy cushions where kids can relax. You can easily while away the afternoon here.

Village Books

751 South Street, Roslindale 617-325-1994 | www.village-books.net

This is my neighborhood bookstore. It's an adorable little shop that focuses on kids' books, but it has a lot of cool educational toys too.

to the Rose Kennedy Greenway. There's a fountain to splash around in if it's hot.

Clarendon Street Playground
At the corner of Clarendon Street and Commonwealth Avenue, Back Bay

No water, but this is a top-notch playground, maintained faithfully by a neighborhood committee. There are various events open to the public (such as a Halloween party) throughout the year—look for postings on the bulletin board. Toys for all kids to use are a friendly touch. It's just a block from busy Newbury Street, and unlike so many playgrounds, it offers loads of shade. If you tire of the playground, a walk on Commonwealth Mall looking at statues and beautiful brownstones can be diverting. Many local preschools and schools use the playground, so it can get crowded.

Langone Park
Commercial Street, North End

This sweet little playground has got one of the best views in town and everything you need for relaxing after an afternoon in the North End. It even has a public bathroom. The playground sits right on the edge (almost) of the Charles River. It's enclosed and has swings and a climbing structure. The fact that you can walk to get some of the best pastries and cappuccinos in the city has nothing to do with it being a favorite. Really.

Stoneman Playground on the Esplanade
Between Fairfield and Massachusetts Avenue, Back Bay

This playground on the Esplanade offers two separate gated areas: one for toddlers and one for older kids. Beside the view, what makes this a special spot is their free Sundays in the Park program. It runs in early May and June and again in September and October from 2pm to 4pm. Anything from music to magic shows to pony rides might be featured. Visit www.esplanadeassociation.org for more details. While I can sometimes get bored at playgrounds, I am content to watch the river for hours.

As our summers seem so fleeting and our winters so long, the city of Boston knows how to make the most of the warm weather by hosting special events and creating fantastic programs that will have you (and more important, the kids) outdoors as much as possible. Here are just a few favorites that are family friendly. (For more events throughout the year, see chapter 10; for a really comprehensive list, visit the Greater Boston Convention and Visitors Bureau website: www.bostonusa.com.)

May

Wake Up the Earth Festival: Held the first Saturday in May, this is a fantastic way to kick off the spring. The non-profit arts and culture group Spontaneous Celebrations throws a big party in Jamaica Plain with music, dance, theatre, arts and crafts, and much more. Visit www.spontaneous-celebrations.org for details.

June

The Jimmy Fund Scooper Bowl: Both a fundraiser and an ice cream lover's dream. All-you-can-eat ice cream on the City Hall Plaza is a messy, delightful treat. Visit www.jimmyfund.org for details.

July & August

Boston Harborfest: A full week of festivities, including the Fourth of July and Boston Pops concert at the Hatch Shell. Visit www.bostonharborfest.com for details.

ParkARTS Program: For several years the city of Boston has sponsored a ParkARTS program in the summer, which features a variety of artists who engage with kids to paint, sculpt, or do other art activities. For a schedule, check the City of Boston Parks & Recreation website, www.cityofboston.gov; Search: ParkARTS. You can playground hop all week and find something different to do at each one.

Parks & Green Spaces

Boston is blessed with a huge variety of green spaces, and luckily we've done our bit to preserve them. The Emerald Necklace—the nine parks linked by parkways and waterways that run though Boston—was designed by Frederick Law Olmsted and connects Boston Common and the Public Garden along the Muddy River and Leverett, Willow, Ward's, and Jamaica ponds through the Arnold Arboretum to Franklin Park. From stopping to smell the flowers to feeding ducks to running around a pond, your kids will love the variety as much as you will. In addition, there are a variety of other places to check out, such as the newly finished Rose Kennedy Greenway and the ever-expanding Harborwalk.

Arnold Arboretum

125 Arborway, Jamaica Plain
617-524-1718 | www.arboretum.harvard.edu
Grounds are open dawn to dusk; Visitor's Center open Monday–Friday, 9AM–4PM; Saturday, 10AM–4PM; Sunday, noon–4PM.

You can bike, in-line skate, run, or just stroll among the walkways in this beautiful 250-acre park. The Arnold Arboretum is a National Historic Landmark and part of Harvard University. This is a wonderful place to bring kids to learn how to ride their bikes. One year my family had an Easter egg hunt here (probably not a sanctioned activity). Lilac Sunday, held the third Sunday in May, is a spectacular time to visit (and the only time you are allowed to picnic on the grounds). If your child likes treasure hunts (or letterboxing) visit the arboretum website and download the Tree-of-the-Month activity guide, which leads you on an adventure through the grounds. Other special programs are offered periodically, so check the website often.

Back Bay Fens

Between Park Drive and The Fenway, Boston
617-522-2700 | www.emeraldnecklace.org

The Back Bay Fens is part of Boston's Emerald Necklace. Its previous life was that of a marsh, which was drained and filled in, and then turned into parkland. It is fun to walk through the Victory Gardens, the nation's oldest remaining WWII gardens. Ask your little critic to contemplate each gardener's personality from their designs. There is also a rose garden, absolutely stunning in bloom, and myriad pathways to explore and, of course, a playground.

Boston Common

Bordered by Tremont, Park, Boylston, and Beacon streets, Boston
617-426-3115

The country's oldest park, established in 1634, was used for grazing livestock, then for hanging criminals, and now happily is just a great place to escape the city sidewalks. The Frog Pond and the Tadpole playground are great for kids, but so is just running around the landscaped paths chasing pigeons and admiring flowers.

Boston Nature Center

500 Walk Hill Street, Mattapan
617-983-8500 | www.massaudubon.org
Nature Center is open Monday–Friday, 9AM–5PM;
Saturday, Sunday, and Monday holidays, 10AM–4PM.
Trails are open from dawn to dusk.
Suggested donation of $2 for nonmembers.

This Mass Audubon property has two miles of wheelchair accessible trails and boardwalks that take you through meadows and wetlands where you might see a number of creatures, from coyotes to all sorts of birds. They offer fantastic summer camps and winter programs, but just looking for animals or checking out the displays in the Nature Center makes for a wonderful excursion.

Franklin Park

Circuit Drive, Dorchester
617-442-4141 | www.franklinparkcoalition.org

While home to the kid-pleasing Franklin Park Zoo, the 527-acre park has even more to offer. This "country park" is the largest park and crown jewel of Olmsted's work on the Emerald Necklace. Named for Benjamin Franklin, the park has six miles of roads and fifteen miles of pedestrian and bridle paths to explore. Take a walk on a two-and-a-half mile loop path through woods or visit one of three playgrounds located on the edges of the park. Check the website for events such as guided walks and festivals.

Jamaica Pond

Jamaicaway, Jamaica Plain
617-522-2700 | www.emeraldnecklace.org; Search: Jamaica Pond

Jamaica Pond, also part of Boston's Emerald Necklace, happens to be the city's reserve water supply—so no swimming! There are plenty of other things to do though. Walk the one-and-a-half mile paved trail, let kids ride their bikes in safety, feed the ducks and geese, fish, or just kick back. You can also rent rowboats and sailboats from the Courageous Sailing Center from April through October (see page 101). Jamaica Pond also is the location for a number of festive but low-key seasonal celebrations, including the Lantern Festival in October.

Paul Revere Park

Constitution Road, Charlestown
617-482-1722 | www.bostonharborwalk.com

This is one of the parks along the Boston Harborwalk. There are five acres to roam and have a picnic; a fenced-in playground; and a great view of the Charles River. Located where the Charles meets the Inner Harbor, the park extends upstream from the North Washington Street Bridge to the Leonard P. Zakim Bunker Hill Bridge. You can even fish off the pier.

Public Garden

Charles Street, Boston
617-723-8144 | www.friendsofthepublicgarden.org

The Public Garden, home to the Swan Boats and the duckling statues, was established in 1837 and is the oldest public botanical garden in the country. Hundreds of species of trees and flowers abound in this beautiful park. It's a luxurious twenty-four acres, right in the heart of the city. Activity is pretty low-key, as no biking or skating is permitted, and in various spaces you're supposed to keep off the grass. But take in the peace and quiet, take a walk over the world's smallest suspension bridge, and relax on a bench near the weeping willows. Little ones love to feed the many ducks in the lagoon and watch the Swan Boats peddle by.

Rose Kennedy Greenway

Waterfront neighborhoods, Boston
617-292-0020 | www.rosekennedygreenway.org

This one mile of parks and green space goes through Chinatown, the Wharf District, and the North End neighborhoods for a total of fifteen acres of parkland in the heart of the city. It's a triumph of green over concrete, as this space was born of the notorious Big Dig. Though there is more work to be done, it's a delight to meander through the city here, offering a much more peaceful trip than you'd expect. There's tons for kids to look at as you go though various neighborhoods. In 2008, there was a wonderful opening celebration with music, art, and performances. Look on the website for similar future festivals and events.

Turtle Pond Parkway, West Roxbury/
Hyde Park
617-333-7404
www.mass.gov/dcr; Search: Stony

This 475-acre green space on the edge of
Boston offers about ten miles of hiking trails and bicycle
paths, plus a playground and a tot lot. You can also fish for
sunfish and perch in Turtle Pond. There are soccer and baseball fields,
tennis courts, picnic areas, an ice-skating rink, and a pool; there is
something to do here all year long.

Barely Beyond Boston: Other Great Outdoor Spaces

BEACHES & PONDS

Breakheart Reservation
177 Forest Street, Saugus
781-233-0834 | www.mass.gov/dcr; Search: Breakheart
Open daily, dawn to dusk.
Free.

Breakheart Reservation is a 640-acre forest with a supervised swimming area at Pearce Lake, one of the few freshwater swimming spots north of Boston. You can hike the trails and even fish. Rangers sometimes conduct family-friendly programs, usually near the lake. Call for more details.

Houghton's Pond
695 Hillside Street, Milton
617-698-1802 | www.mass.gov/dcr; Search: Houghton's Pond
Open daily, dawn to dusk.
DCR lifeguards on duty July–August, daily, 10AM–6PM.

Somehow in all my years in Boston, I never knew anything about Houghton's Pond. A few years ago, my daughter attended a summer birthday party there, and really, it is one of the best outings in the area. The pond is a spring-fed kettle hole that is a massive twenty-four acres. There's a supervised swimming beach, stocked fishing, picnic tables (reserve in advance), three ball fields, and a playground. A concession pavilion and visitor's center are open in the summer, as are restrooms and a first aid station. If anyone in the family doesn't like muck on their feet, bring water shoes. It is a pond after all. The good news is the water gets much warmer here than in the Atlantic.

Walden Pond State Reservation

915 Walden Street, Concord
978-369-3254 | www.mass.gov/dcr; Search: Walden
Open daily, 5AM to dusk.
Admission is $5 per car.

Get here early to stake your claim (and parking space) at Henry David Thoreau's former backyard. Lifeguards (in season) parole a roped-off area on a small beach where most families park themselves. The shallow water extends for several feet and allows little ones to splash around in safety. You can swim beyond the ropes if you want, but they make a good boundary for the children. A bathhouse makes changing clothes convenient. The only food around is an ice cream truck conveniently located in the parking lot, so be sure to bring food and water if you'll be staying for the day.

WADING POOLS, SPRAY DECKS & POOLS

Department of Conservation and Recreation

617-727-5290 | www.mass.gov/dcr

The following facilities are run by the Department of Conservation and Recreation (DCR). Most spray pools are open from dawn to dusk. DCR pools offer free admission, but make sure you call to check on hours and maintenance.

Of all these, the Veterans Memorial Swimming and Wading Pool has lots to offer—a river view, changing rooms, showers, parking, a playground nearby, and lifeguards on duty.

Dilboy Memorial Swimming and Wading Pool
Alewife Brook Parkway, Somerville

Latta Brothers Memorial Swimming and Wading Pool
McGrath Highway, Somerville

McCrehan Memorial Swimming and Wading Pool
359 Rindge Avenue, Cambridge

Veterans Memorial Swimming and Wading Pool
Magazine Beach, 719 Memorial Drive, Cambridge

Parks & Playgrounds

There are so many playgrounds and parks in the Boston area, I could easily fill up volumes with details, but I'll just give you my top picks. To find all the playgrounds and parks in Brookline, visit the Parks and Open Space Department website, www.brooklinema.gov/parks, or call 617-730-2088. Their excellent website gives very detailed specs on every park in town. For information on Newton parks, visit www.ci.newton.ma.us/parks or call 617-796-1500.

Blue Hills Reservation

695 Hillside Street, Milton
617-698-1802 | www.mass.gov/dcr; Search: Blue Hills Reservation
Blue Hill Meteorological Observatory is open February–November, Saturday–Sunday, late morning to mid-afternoon.
Adults, $3; children 5–17, $1.50.

There's plenty to occupy families at the Blue Hills Reservation, which encompasses more than seven thousand acres from Quincy to Dedham, Milton to Randolph. Almost every outdoor activity from hiking, biking, and rock climbing to fishing, swimming, and more can be done here. Several events are held annually at the Blue Hill Meteorological Observatory, located at the top of Great Blue Hill. Founded in 1885, it is the oldest continually operating weather record in the country. Tours of the observatory are offered as weather permits. It is a hike to get there, but you'll learn about meteorology, weather instruments, and get a great view. See Houghton's Pond listing for swimming information.

Larz Anderson Park

Bounded by Newton Street, Avon Street, and Goddard Avenue, Brookline
617-730-2069 | www.townofbrooklinemass.com

Larz Anderson Park, with sixty-four acres, has everything one could hope for in a park: an excellent playground, a picnic table area, barbecue pits, a pond, and an outdoor ice-skating rink and sports fields. Don't miss the Temple of Love pavilion sitting on the edge of the lagoon. It's a pleasant spot to sit. The views of Boston from the hilltop are amazing. In the summer, you can have a fabulous cookout or picnic if you reserve in advance. My daughter's elementary school has an annual picnic here, as do many large groups—so start planning.

Weezie's Garden
900 Washington Street (Route 16), Wellesley
617-933-4900 | www.masshort.org

This fun children's garden at the Massachusetts Horticultural Society's Elm Bank is designed as a series of small spiraling gardens, each with its own theme and different ways of engaging the senses. Each smaller spiral gives kids the opportunity to plant, water, or interact in some way with the garden's elements. Children's activities are held throughout the spring, summer, and fall.

Winthrop Square (Minot Rose Garden)
St. Paul Street, Brookline

This fantastic playground has a variety of structures, a spray area, swings, a water fountain (why don't all playgrounds have these?), and the adjacent beautiful Minot Rose Garden. Kids delight in going back and forth between the two.

◆7 Great Getaways & Day Trips

OKAY, YOU'VE HAD enough of the city. You want to strap the baby into the car seat and take a drive to explore something new. (Maybe the little one will even nap!)

I've picked my favorites and organized them by month to provide some inspiration at a glance. Say it's the middle of February and you're stumped on what to do with your little angel (who's fast becoming your little devil): head to Providence and check out its amazing Children's Museum. Or possibly it's the hottest day of the year—and it just so happens that it's in May: head to World's End, where you can partake in a seaside picnic complete with a refreshing ocean breeze.

I've also included a couple alternatives for each month. Of course, most of these spots would be fine any time of the year, but some are better than others in different seasons, and some are only open for limited months. Many of these outings are great for playgroups looking for a change of pace, and none of these trips are more than a two-hour drive from Boston.

Discovery Museums

177 Main Street, Acton
978-264-4200 | www.discoverymuseums.org
Call or visit the website for hours; the schedule depends on the
season and special events.

Science and Children's museums, $13; one museum, $9.
Adults and children pay the same price; children under 3 at Science
Museum, $5; under 1, free.

After the excitement of the winter holidays has died down and you're
at your wit's end trying to figure out something to do outside of the
house (no more *Sesame Street!*), this is just the ticket. Without a doubt,
your toddler-aged child will want to visit both museums, so buy the
double pass up front. If you're toting an infant, you'll probably just stick
to the smaller Children's Museum.

The ten exhibits in the Children's Museum, which occupies a Victorian
house, explore different themes. There's the Train Room, Bessie's Play
Diner, Woodland Room, and several other fanciful delights designed
for younger children. Those with infants should head straight for the
Sensations Room, designed especially for babies.

While the Science Museum is really best suited to older children,
preschoolers love it too. There's an Inventor's Workshop, Music Room,
Earth Science Room, and a great deal more to check out.

TIP: There's a no food/drink policy here. You either can eat in your car
(yeah, right) or head into Acton.

Other Great Getaways

Cape Cod Children's Museum

577 Great Neck Road South, Mashpee
508-539-8788 | www.capecodchildrensmuseum.org
September-May, Tuesday-Thursday, 10AM-3PM;
Friday-Saturday until 5PM; Sunday, noon-5PM; Memorial Day-Labor
Day, Tuesday-Saturday, 10AM-5PM; Sunday, noon-5PM.
Admission is $6.

With its hands-on exhibits, a pirate ship, and an indoor planetarium,
this museum is not just for rainy vacation days!

55 Coogan Boulevard, Mystic, CT
860-572-5955 | www.mysticaquarium.org
March 1–October 31, daily, 9AM–6PM; November, daily, 9AM–5PM;
December–February, daily, 10AM–5PM.
Last admission one hour before closing.
Adults, $26; children 3–17, $19; under 2, free.

You won't need to get wet to meet Mystic's ocean animals, including Boomerang the sea lion pup, star of the live show!

February

Providence Children's Museum

100 South Street, Providence, RI
401-273-5437 | www.childrenmuseum.org
September–March, Tuesday–Sunday, 9AM–6PM;
April–Labor Day, daily, 9AM–6PM.
Admission is $7.50; under 12 months, free.
If you are an annual member at the Boston Children's Museum, you have reciprocal privileges here (so it's free).

Despite being so close, it's easy to forget that Providence is an easy option for families looking for a change of pace. You can get to the Children's Museum in less than an hour, and it's worth the trip. The Littlewoods exhibit is limited to children under age four with a caregiver. There are balls to play with, small slides, costumes, and puppets. Books and other resources for parents are provided too. Older kids will want to explore the Water Ways exhibit, where they can—and will—get wet. They will also love the Shape Space exhibit, chock full of blocks and other building materials, as well as the newest exhibit called Play Power. Activities include open-ended play with music, air, sound, and construction.

Tip: There is a lunchroom where you can eat your own lunch. There is no restaurant on site, so head out if you didn't brown bag it.

Children's Museum in Easton

9 Sullivan Avenue, North Easton
508-230-3789 | www.childrensmuseumineaston.org
Tuesday-Friday, 9AM-5PM; Saturday-Sunday, noon-5PM.
Admission is $6; under 1, free.

Complete with a fire pole, a kid's camp, and performance area, this charming museum in an old fire station is a big hit!

Dover Children's Museum

6 Washington Street, Dover, NH
603-742-2002 | www.childrens-museum.org
Tuesday-Saturday, 10AM-5PM; Sunday, noon-5PM.
Admission is $7; under 1, free.

This museum offers great hands-on exhibits, including the Step into the Story exhibit—where the pages of your child's favorite picture books spring to life around them.

March

Drumlin Farm Wildlife Sanctuary

208 South Great Road, Route 117, Lincoln
781-259-2200 | www.massaudubon.org/drumlinfarm
March-October, Tuesday-Sunday and Monday holidays, 9AM-5PM;
November-February, 9AM-4PM.
Adults, $6; children 3-12, $4; free to Mass Audubon Society members.

The Massachusetts Audubon Society runs this 250-acre working farm, which is the darling home to pigs, cows, horses, and a chicken coop beyond compare. In addition to the old favorites, there is the Burrowing Animal Building—complete with foxes and woodchucks—trails to explore, and gardens to poke around in. A gift shop and small farm stand are located near the entrance.

Drumlin Farm offers programs and demonstrations throughout the year, but I like to visit in March because it's maple sugar season. On special days you can help collect sap from a sugar bush and visit the evaporator where it boils down. The annual Sap-to-Syrup Farmer's Breakfast happens twice in March—a special treat when you actually get to eat the tasty stuff!

Other activities that are worth checking out include the See How It Grew program, where kids and their parents help put the farm's garden to rest in the winter; and the Farmers' Helper program, where kids assist in milking the cows, collecting eggs, and other charming farmyard chores.

Tip: If you can brave the March weather, there are picnic tables for lunch.

Other Great Getaways

Ecotarium

222 Harrington Way, Worcester
508-929-2700 | www.ecotarium.org
Tuesday–Saturday, 10AM–5PM; Sunday, noon–5PM.
Adults, $10; children 3–18, $8; under 3, free.

This unique indoor-outdoor museum offers a chance to walk through the treetops, take a thrilling multimedia journey, meet wildlife, and ride a narrow-gauge railroad. The polar bear is worth the trip alone!

New England's Butterfly Conservatory and Gardens Magic Wings

281 Greenfield Road, South Deerfield
413-665-2805 | www.magicwings.com
September–May, 9AM–5PM; June–August, 9AM–6PM.
Adults, $12; children 3–17, $8; under 2, free.

The 8,000-square foot conservatory is filled with butterflies, moths, and tropical vegetation; if that isn't enough to warm the spirit, stop by the fieldstone fireplace to warm up.

April

Garden in the Woods

180 Hemenway Road, Framingham
508-877-7630 | www.newenglandwildflower.org/garden.htm
April 15–July 3, Tuesday–Sunday and Monday holidays, 9AM–5PM;
Thursday and Friday until 7PM;
July 6–October 31, Tuesday–Sunday and Monday holidays, 9AM–5PM.
Adults, $8; children 3–18, $4.

I can't think of a better place to spend Earth Day, or any nice spring day for that matter, than at the forty-five-acre Garden in the Woods. The garden opens its doors for free on Earth Day in celebration, and there are special activities and programs. There are more than a thousand native plant species, with landscaped paths and walkways to explore, and it makes for a delightful wander. You can take an informal guided tour (kids welcome) to learn all about what you are looking at Tuesdays through Fridays at 10am and on weekends at 2pm. Tours are offered at 10am on Monday holidays when the garden is open too.

Tip: Special children's programs are offered year-round. Kids can make a garbage garden, learn about frogs, or go on a turtle trek. Visit the website for details.

Other Great Getaways

Hancock Shaker Village

34 Lebanon Mt. Road, Hancock
413-443-0188 | www.hsv.lsw.com
Self-guided tours, mid-April–mid-May, 10AM–4PM; mid-May–mid-October, 10AM–5PM. The rest of the year, guided tours are required. Call ahead.
Adults, $16.50; children 13–17, $8; under 12, free.

The village comes to life through exhibitions, demonstrations, and participatory activities. Kids can even take a lesson with a Shaker schoolteacher.

Stony Brook Wildlife Sanctuary

108 North Street, Norfolk
508-528-3140 | www.massaudubon.org
Nature Center: Tuesday–Friday, 9AM–5PM; Saturday–Sunday, 10AM–4PM; July–August, also open Monday, 9AM–5PM.
Trails: Daily, dawn to dusk.
Adults, $4; children 2–12, $3.

Follow the boardwalk along the edge of Teal Marsh for views of turtles, fish, muskrats, and great blue herons. In the summer, be on the lookout for the buzz of activity in the butterfly garden by the nature center.

May

World's End

250 Martins Lane, Hingham
781-740-6665 | www.thetrustees.org
Daily, 8AM–dusk.
Adults, $5; under 12, free.

Family membership is $65 (which allows you access to ninety-nine properties in Massachusetts).

The Trustees of Reservations, like Mass Audubon, is a non-profit organization dedicated to preserving special places. World's End was once destined to be a housing development, but it never happened. Before the project was derailed though, Frederick Law Olmstead landscaped the grounds. The paths and walkways remain, but there are no houses to spoil the view. The property is part of the Boston Harbor Islands national park area. Hiking and walking are the main activities on the 200-plus-acre peninsula. Archaeologists think that the site was a seasonal campsite for Native Americans.

The Trustees offer a variety of programs at World's End for families with children of varying ages. The Family Outing options include one for adults with kids ages two to three or one for adults with kids ages four to five. If you don't want to join a program, the 4.5-miles of trails to explore are ample diversion. Call or check their website to learn more about the events they offer throughout the year.

Tip: This is no place for a stroller. Bring a kiddie backpack for the small ones. Plan on picnicking.

Other Great Getaways

Capron Park Zoo
201 County Street, Attleboro
774-203-1840 | www.capronparkzoo.com
November–March, daily, 10AM–4PM; April–October, daily, 10AM–5PM.
Last ticket sold one hour before closing.
Adults, $5.50; children 3–12, $3.75; under 2, free.

Great things come in pint-sized packages at this fabulous zoo. Combined with an award-winning playground, this zoo is sure to delight your little animals.

Weir River Farm
Turkey Hill Lane, Hingham
781-784-0567 | www.thetrustees.org
Daily, dawn to dusk.
Free.

A Trustees of Reservations property where you can take a 1.5-mile loop through the grounds of a former estate.

June

Southwick's Zoo

2 Southwick Street, Mendon
508-883-9182 | www.southwickszoo.com
Mid-April–mid-October, daily, 10AM–5PM.
*Adults, $18.75; children 3–12, $12.75; combo ticket,
which includes mechanical rides, $24.*

By size and by numbers, this is the largest zoo in New England. Prices are a little steep because it's privately owned (go online to print a coupon or bring your AAA card for a discount). Like Davis Farmland, the Southwick's Zoo was once a real working farm. Prepare to spend a full day here because that's the only way you'll even see half of the animals on the 175 acres; chances are, you'll probably get caught up attending the presentations and shows offered throughout the day. The thirty-five-acre deer forest is a great exhibit. Buy feed and stroll through the forest; the deer will come eat right out of your hand!

Southwick's Zoo is also more than just a showcase for animals. Earth Limited operates from the zoo, educating the public about environmentalism and animal ecology. Animal rides (pony, camel, or elephant) and mechanical rides (carousel, train, etc.) will beckon your child (and cost a little extra). Though the zoo has a limited season, be sure to log on to the Zookeeper's Diary online so you can find out when babies are born and view photos of the animals.

Tip: The zoo has seven different food venues offering everything from pizza to salads to sandwiches.

Other Great Getaways

Buttonwood Zoo

425 Hawthorn Street, New Bedford
508-991-6178 | www.bpzoo.org
Daily, 10AM–5PM. Last entry at 4:30PM.
Adults, $6; children 3–12, $3; under 2, free.

Discover the animals in your own backyard! With a few exceptions, all of the animals carry out the zoo's theme, "From the Berkshires to the Sea."

Roger Williams Park Zoo

1000 Elmwood Avenue, Providence, RI
401-785-3510 | www.rogerwilliamsparkzoo.org
Daily, 9AM–4PM. Last entry at 3:30PM.
Adults, $12; children 3–12, $6; under 2, free.

From the giraffes to the elephants—Roger Williams Park Zoo is a must-visit attraction!

July

Walden Pond State Reservation

915 Walden Street, Concord
978-369-3254 | www.mass.gov/dcr; Search: Walden
Daily, 5AM to dusk.
$5 per car.

This has always been one of my absolute favorite warm-weather day trips. But come summer, Walden Pond may as well be called Mother's Pond, as it fills up very quickly with moms and kids—so be warned, get here too late and you'll be out of luck. When the parking lot is full, no one else is allowed in. So arrive early, bring your lunch and an umbrella, and prepare to relax. Swimming in Henry David Thoreau's former backyard is a joy for parents and their children. Lifeguards (in season) parole a roped-off area on a small beach where most families park themselves. The shallow water extends for several feet and allows little ones to splash around in safety. You can swim beyond the ropes if you want, but they make a good boundary for the children. If you want to get out of the water, take a walk around the pond.

A bathhouse makes changing clothes convenient. The only

food around is an ice cream truck conveniently located in the parking lot, so be sure to bring food and water if you'll be staying for the day. Occasionally, the park rangers host activities for children outside the water. They include nature crafts, story time, and a Junior Ranger series. Adult and family activities include poetry readings, tracking programs, and Thoreau walks. Call for details and dates of various events.

Tip: Although the pond has a lot of shade, it's all away from the beach area. Bring an umbrella.

Explore the Great Outdoors

Forest Hills Cemetery
617-524-0128 | www.foresthillstrust.org
What, take the kids to a cemetery? Absolutely! The Forest Hills Cemetery, established in 1848, is a beautiful place to take children. Though it is still an active burial ground, it is also a historic site, an open-air museum, and a 275-acre park. Walk along the Contemporary Sculpture Path, an ongoing exhibition of sculptures laid out along a one-mile route. Diverse works of sculpture by local and national artists form a route through the oldest part of the grounds, around Lake Hibiscus, and into the newest sections. The memorial sculptures are always beautiful, and you can pick up a map to take a self-guided tour. Check the website for family concerts and other events throughout the year.

Mass Audubon
800-283-8266 | www.massaudubon.org
Annual family membership is $58
Hands down, this is one of the best organizations to join, other than the library, and a bargain to boot. Once you have a baby, getting out of the house is a requirement. Mass Audubon has forty-five wildlife sanctuaries, where you can do everything from nature hikes to skiing to story hours. The non-profit cares for 33,000 acres of conservation land and includes the Boston Nature Center, Blue Hills Reservation, and Drumlin Farm, among many others. Your annual membership gives you access to all the sanctuaries. Many of the events held year-round are free or discounted for members.

Other Great Getaways

Kimball Farm

400 Littleton Road, Westford
978-486-3891 | www.kimballfarm.com
Ice cream stand: Daily, 10AM–9PM.
Mini golf course and bumper boats: Monday–Thursday, 10AM–7PM;
Friday–Sunday, 10AM–9PM, weather permitting.

Mini golf: Adults, $11; 12 and under, $8.50.

Bumper boats: $7.50 per person.

Combo ticket: Adults, $17; under 12, $14.50.

From homemade ice cream to a country store and bumper boats, this family farm is the perfect antidote to a hot summer day in the city.

Strawbery Banke Museum

14 Hancock Street, Portsmouth, NH
603-433-1100 | www.strawberybanke.org
May–October, daily, 10AM–5PM.
Call or visit website for December hours.

Adults, $15; children 5–17, $10; under 4, free;
family ticket (for two adults and two children), $40.

Discover an interactive experience that opens a window onto the past. The Victorian Garden features a tea garden, plants that tell time, a butterfly and fairy garden, and a two-story naturalistic Victorian tree house.

August

Davis Farmland & Maze

145 Redstone Hill, Sterling
978-422-8888 | www.davisfarmland.com
www.davismegamaze.com

Farmland: Weather permitting, April 16–Labor Day, daily, 9:30AM; September 10–October 18, Thursday–Sunday; October 18–November 1, Saturday–Sunday. Closing hours vary; call for times.

Maze: August 6–September 7, daily, 10AM–6PM; September 11–October 31, weekends only, 10AM–6PM; November 1–15, weekends only, 10AM–5PM.

Mega Maze: Weather permitting, mid-July to early September; October, Saturday–Sunday. The opening dates depend upon the crop, so call to find out.

Farmland admission: $13.95; June 13–Labor Day, $16.95; under 2, free.

This place is worth a whole day. If you have a mixed-age group, you can visit both the Farmland and the Mega Maze, but you'll need a full day to do both. The complex is run by the seventh generation of the Davis family. When farming wasn't making money for them anymore, they turned the land into a more profitable venture.

The Farmland is the perfect size for your pint-sized adventurer. Although the Farmland caters to kids under eight years, older siblings will like the animals too. Children are encouraged to go right into most of the animal pens. The farm is more than a mere petting zoo though: it is home to many rare species of livestock, which the Davis's are breeding to save from extinction.

The Mega Maze is definitely geared more for adults and older kids. It's an amazing example of what you can do with a tractor and a cornfield. Each year a master maze maker from England redesigns the maze, and it takes on a new theme. One year it was Lost Vegas. The following year it was Olympic Rings. In 2009, it was the Lost Tomb. Make sure your kids are up for the challenge though—it can be a little claustrophobic, and being stuck in a cornfield with a screaming toddler is no fun. Stick to the Farmland if you think that might be a problem.

Tip: Be sure to pack bathing suits, towels, and sunscreen. There's a huge Play & Spray area to cool down in. There is a concession stand and picnic area, so brown bag it or bring some extra cash.

Other Great Getaways

Fort Adams

Fort Adams State Park, Newport, RI
401-841-0707 | www.fortadams.org
Memorial Day–Columbus Day, 10AM–4PM.
The only way to visit is by tour, given on the hour.
*Adults, $10; children 6–17, $5; under 5, free;
family rate, $25 (two adults and up to four youths).*

The largest coastal fortification in the United States, where you can see where the soldiers lived. Enter the casemates, explore the tunnel system, and climb the bastions, plus relax and have a picnic—curious little explorers will love it.

302 Sumner Avenue, Springfield
413-733-2251 | www.forestparkzoo.org
Weather permitting, March 29–October 13, daily, 10AM–5PM;
October 13–November 30, Saturday–Sunday, 10AM–3:30PM.
Adults, $6; children 5–12, $4; children 1–4, $2; under 1, free.

Dedicated to wildlife education, with different events almost every weekend that focus on science and animals, plus story times.

September

Parlee Farms

95 Farwell Road, Tyngsboro
978-649-3854 | www.parleefarm.com
June–August, generally Tuesday–Sunday, 8AM–6PM;
September–October, Tuesday–Sunday, 10AM–5PM.
Call ahead to check days and hours, which vary depending on activity.
Call for rates.

Parlee Farms makes a delightful low-key family outing, with something for everyone: a variety of fruits and flowers for picking, a clean and well-arranged farm animal petting zoo, a fun Hay Play Area, a demonstration beehive, and an attractive farm stand.

Annie's Animal Barn features two barns filled with young farm animals you can feed and even pet. There are goats, sheep, bunnies, and chickens. Most of the animals (not the chickens!) will eat right out of your hand. There is a goat walk where you can send goat food to a high platform to feed the goats, a big hit with the kids (of both species).

September is perfect for picking apples and pumpkins. There are free hayrides to over fourteen-acres of apple orchards. In addition, through September, you can pick and cut your own flowers. The farm has more than a dozen colors of gladiolus, various shades of zinnias, as well as sunflowers and dahlias.

Other Great Getaways

89 Pleasant Street South, South Natick
508-653-0653 | www.lookoutfarm.com
Early May–August, Saturday–Sunday, 10AM–5PM;
August 10–late October, daily, 10AM–5PM.
Petting zoo: September–October.
Admission is $8; under 2, free.

Besides pick your own fruit, there's a terrific play area, train ride, pony rides, and other activities that will tucker you out long before your little one gets tired.

Honey-Pot Hill Orchards

144 Sudbury Road, Stow
978-562-5666 | www.honeypothill.com
Late July–late October. Call ahead to check days and hours.
Call for rates.

Blueberry, peach, and apple picking, plus hayrides and a hedge maze. If you're looking for the apple-picking experience of your youth, you've found it!

October

Peabody Essex Museum

161 Essex Street, Salem
978-745-9500 | www.pem.org
Tuesday–Sunday and Monday holidays, 10AM–5PM.
Adults, $15; under 16, free.

Besides being an overall fabulous museum packed with more than 800,000 works of art—much of it from merchants who sailed the world and returned with treasures—the museum seriously wants children to turn into lifelong museum-goers. Why else would they have bi-weekly story hours for toddlers; drop-in art activities every weekend for all ages; and many other programs targeted for children and families weekly? Don't miss the Art & Nature Center, where families can enjoy changing exhibitions and hands-on displays.

There are, gulp, thirty galleries to explore, but the gorgeous and interesting exhibit Yin Yu Tang: A Chinese House never fails to fascinate kids. This 200-year-old Chinese merchant's home was taken from China and reassembled at the museum (it's an extra $5 admission for adults).

Tip: Since I am recommending this as an October day trip, leave some extra time to explore downtown Salem, which will be decorated to the hilt for Halloween.

Other Great Getaways

DeCordova Museum & Sculpture Park

51 Sandy Pond Road, Lincoln
781-259-8355 | www.decordova.org
Galleries: Tuesday–Sunday, 10AM–5PM.
Sculpture Garden: Daily, dawn to dusk.
Adults, $12; children 6–12, $8; under 5, free.
When the galleries are closed, admission to the sculpture park is free.

What could be better than an outdoor art adventure? Pack a lunch and make a day of it. Also check out the Family Activity Kit at the front desk of the museum. For older kids, look into the Eye Wonder program, which celebrates contemporary artists and their work processes with family-friendly tours and art activities.

Hammond Castle Museum

80 Hesperus Avenue, Gloucester
978-283-2080 | www.hammondcastle.org
May–October, Saturday–Sunday, 10AM–4PM. Last entry at 3:30PM.
Adults, $10; children 6–12, $6; under 5, free.

Traipse through a medieval-style castle! There's even a secret passage to explore.

November

Plimoth Plantation & the Mayflower II

137 Warren Avenue, Plymouth
508-746-1622 | www.plimoth.org
Plantation: March–November, daily, 9:30AM–5PM
(some exhibit hours vary).
Mayflower II: Daily, 9AM–5PM.
Plantation only: Adults, $24; children 6–12, $14.
Mayflower II only: Adults, $10; children 6–12, $7; under 5, free.
Combo pass (good for two days): Adults, $28; children 6–12, $18.

PLIMOTH PLANTATION

Visit the year 1627 in this re-creation of a Pilgrim village (about twenty structures) and Hobbamock's (Wampanoag Indian) Homesite. Trained staff dress and speak as though they were in the seventeenth century. This living history museum is a great way to impart an important part of our past. The staff can tell you how they cook on a hearth or how difficult the winters are, all in period dialect. In Hobbamock's Homesite (where interpreters speak modern-day English), you can watch a canoe being built or visit the *wetuash* (houses). Hobbamock was a Pokanoket Indian and Plymouth Colony's interpreter and guide. Older children and adults will get more out of this museum than smaller children, at least from a learning perspective, but don't write it off for toddlers. Playing dress up is huge deal to little kids, and to be plunked down in a space where all the grown-ups are playacting is thrilling for little ones. Also, since much of the museum has you wandering in the outdoors, kids who want to run around or who get bored inside easily will be happy.

MAYFLOWER II

The Mayflower II is part of the museum complex, although it is located on the Plymouth waterfront. This re-creation of the original Mayflower that brought the Pilgrims to New England is an impressive replica. You'll find on board costumed interpreters more than willing to tell you how hard sailing over the ocean was in 1620. There are exhibits placed right outside the ship explaining why the Pilgrims left England, which native people they encountered on arrival, and which navigation techniques they used. Kids will enjoy participating in games that their seventeenth century counterparts played.

Tip: Reservations are taken in June for the plantation's hugely popular Thanksgiving dinners. If you miss out, there are other Pilgrim dinners in the fall. Check the website for details.

Other Great Getaways

Higgins Armory
100 Barber Avenue, Worcester
508-853-6015 | www.higgins.org
Tuesday-Saturday, 10AM-4PM; Sunday, noon-4PM.
Adults, $9; children 6–16, $7; under 5, free.

The only museum in the Northeast entirely devoted to the study and display of arms and armor. It is housed in a Gothic castle with thousands of artifacts.

Wenham Museum

132 Main Street, Wenham
978-468-2377 | www.wenhammuseum.org
Tuesday–Sunday, 10AM–4PM.
Adults, $7; children 2 and up, $5.

The Wenham Museum has a world-famous doll and toy collection and model train gallery. Kids love the Family Discovery Gallery with an interactive space, including a period playhouse, general store, building blocks, doll house, and musical instruments. Save time to visit the Wenham Tea House nearby.

December

Old Sturbridge Village

1 Old Sturbridge Village Road, Route 20, Sturbridge
508-347-3362 | www.osv.org
April–October, daily, 9:30AM–5PM;
October–March, Tuesday–Sunday, 9:30AM–4PM. Special hours for school breaks and holidays; call or visit website for details.
Adults, $20; children 3–17, $7; under 2, free. Tickets are good for two visits within 10 days.

I know—two living history museums back to back? But wait, there's a reason. Since Plimoth Plantation has lots of fun activities focusing on the Pilgrims, it makes sense to go in November (at least to me). Sturbridge is permanently set in the years 1790 to 1840 (Plimoth Plantation is set in 1627) and can be visited year-round. But for my money, it's magical in the winter, with free sleigh rides given on the weekends and festive holiday decorations.

The property is very large, with more than forty buildings, plus animals, and lots of hands-on activities. It usually has a lot going on, so you're bound to find something to entertain the kids, no matter their age. When you get your ticket, you'll receive a map and a list of that day's events. After an orientation program, you can plan the rest of your visit. You'll definitely need at least a few hours. The Samson's Children's Museum should be the first stop for those with smaller children. A dress-up area, play kitchen, and schoolroom are all inviting places to play and are an exciting way to learn about the past.

There are plenty of choices for eating, from a cafeteria to a tavern to a café. On the day you visit you may be able to watch a nineteenth century magic show or drop in for games at the Town Pound. For additional fees, there are hands-on activities for children, such as making wood toys or learning how to stencil. You don't have to get too hung up on planning unless there is something specific you want to do. There is usually a variety of options on any given day.

Tip: The Christmas by Candlelight program runs in December on select evenings and is a blast: twinkling lights, sleigh rides, and caroling will get the kids in the holiday spirit.

Other Great Getaways

Battleship Cove
5 Water Street, Fall River
508-678-1100 | www.battleshipcove.com
Daily, 9AM–5PM.
Adults, $14; children 6–12, $8; under 5, free.

Bring your little sailor to the world's largest naval ship exhibit.

New Bedford Whaling Museum
18 Johnny Cake Hill, New Bedford
508-997-0046 | www.whalingmuseum.org
June–December, daily, 9AM–5PM; January–May, daily, 9AM–4PM;
every second Thursday of the month, open until 9PM.
Adults, $10; children 6–14, $6; under 5, free.

You'd be surprised by how much small children can get out of this beautiful and interesting museum; the whale skeletons are fascinating!

◆ 8 Child Care & Preschool

FOR MANY MOTHERS (and dads too), the question of returning to work after having a child is an area fraught with stress and uncertainty.

It seems like the debate is endless. On any given day you could easily see a segment about working and stay-at-home parents on the news, and then overhear the same debate at your local coffee shop. This is a complicated, nuanced issue that comes down to what's best for a single family.

Whether you choose to return to work, you feel compelled to, or you decide to stay at home altogether, the underlying predicament is the notion that no one could possibly take care of your child as well as you. While there is a certain truth in that, you can also rest assured that there are qualified, caring professionals who have made it their business to provide your child with a level of love and care that may not be as fierce as mom and dad's, but is warm and tender nonetheless.

Choosing appropriate child care is difficult, in part, because there are so many options. From tiny home-centered programs to the local Y, from large franchise programs such as Bright Horizons to a single, dedicated caregiver who comes to your home—there are literally thousands of options to choose from, and what works best for one family may not work for another. A good place to start, as always, is your family, friends, and colleagues. Conduct an independent survey among your network—and, after hearing what they have to say, don't be afraid to scrap every piece of advice they give you and trust your own instincts. As with all things related to parenting, your instincts are the only compass you really need. Also, whatever your child care needs are at the moment, keep in mind that they can and often do change.

In order to help make sense of it all, this chapter includes tips and resources from child care experts. While there are no listings for daycares in this chapter (there are just too many to include), these resources should provide you with a basis for evaluation. In the "Who's Who in Child Care Resources" section, many of the listed organizations offer databases you can search for appropriate child care. At the very least, this chapter will help you discern what you're looking for in a child care provider and how to determine who is qualified to take care of your child. If you are considering a babysitter, nanny, or au pair instead of a daycare, see the resource section in chapter 10. Another great place to begin your search is in the *Boston Parents Paper* magazine. The *Boston Parents Paper* has a great online parent resource center (www.bostonparentspaper.com), as does the online family magazine www.BostonCentral.com.

In many ways, preschool is a less frightening proposition than daycare. Your child can walk, talk, tell you what she needs—maybe she can even go to the bathroom by herself (oh, happy day!). All this said, preschool can be difficult to get into. There are visits and applications; if you are applying in Boston, be prepared for rejections and waitlists. Although there are many great choices in the city, there tends to be more kids than preschool seats. To help focus your search, I've included a list of secular Boston preschools, with class size, tuition, teacher-to-student ratio, and educational philosophies. I've also given resources on finding preschools in surrounding towns. There are a number of excellent preschools with religious affiliations; if this is what your family is looking for, try beginning your search with your own place of worship. Additional information for non-secular programs may be found below in "Who's Who in Child Care Resources." Keep in mind that many non-secular daycares and preschools are open to families of all faiths. Other sources can be found in chapter 10 under "School Resources."

Who's Who in Child Care Resources

Archdiocese of Boston
www.bostoncatholic.org

You can do a search here through a comprehensive directory for Catholic preschools.

Child Care Aware
800-424-2246 | www.childcareaware.org

Child Care Aware helps parents find information on locating quality child care and child care resources in the community by connecting parents with the local agencies. Child Care Aware is a program of the National Association of Child Care Resource & Referral Agencies (NACCRRA).

Child Care Choices of Boston (CCCB)
617-542-5437 | www.childcarechoicesofboston.org

CCCB is the Child Care Resource and Referral Agency (CCRA) for Boston, Chelsea, Winthrop, Revere, and Brookline. Call or visit their website for more information.

JCC Early Learning Centers
617-558-6423 | www.jccearlylearning.org

The Jewish Community Centers of Greater Boston (JCCGB) has six JCC Early Learning Centers in the Greater Boston area: Acton, Brookline, Hingham, Newton, Stoughton/Sharon, and Wayland. Each offers an educational environment based on Derekh Eretz, a Hebrew term for a code of behavior where everyone is treated with respect. The centers share a philosophy and curriculum, but each has a different personality, hours, and tuition. They are open to families and teachers with any amount of Jewish or non-Jewish background. Shabbat is celebrated every week, and many classrooms incorporate simple Hebrew words, phrases, and songs into the day. Jewish holidays are celebrated enthusiastically, as are secular preschool themes such as Seasons, Animals,

A Parent's Guide to Choosing Safe & Healthy Child Care

Supervision

Are children supervised at all times, even when they are sleeping?

Hand Washing and Diapering

Do all caregivers and children wash their hands often, especially before and after eating, using the bathroom, and changing diapers?

Director Qualifications

Does the director of a child care center have a bachelor's degree in a child-related field?

Lead Teacher Qualifications

Does the lead teacher in a child care center have a bachelor's degree in a child-related field? Has the teacher worked in child care for at least one year?

Child Staff Ratio and Group Size

How many children are being cared for in the child care center? The younger the children are, the more caregivers there should be.

Immunizations

Does the child care program have records proving that all children in care are up-to-date on all their required immunizations?

Toxic Substances

Are toxic substances like cleaning supplies and pest killers kept away from children?

Tips and Guidelines

Below you'll find some fantastic tips produced by the National Resource Center for Health and Safety in Child Care for choosing a quality place for your child. You can copy what's here or go online and print out copies. I suggest printing a copy for every center you visit and taking notes during your visit or immediately after. This way you'll have a record of your impressions when you start to review your options.

Emergency Plan

Does the child care program have an emergency plan if a child is injured, sick, or lost? Does the child care program have information about who to contact in an emergency?

Fire Drills

Does the child care program have a plan in case of a disaster like a fire, tornado, flood, blizzard, or earthquake?

Child Abuse

Can caregivers be seen by others at all times, so a child is never alone with one caregiver? Have all caregivers been trained how to prevent child abuse, how to recognize signs of child abuse, and how to report suspected child abuse?

Medications

Does the child care program keep medication out of reach from children?

Staff Training and First Aid

Have caregivers been trained how to keep children healthy and safe from injury and illness?

Playgrounds

Is the playground inspected often for safety? Are the soil and playground surfaces checked often for dangerous substances and hazards?

or Space. The centers are closed on some Jewish holidays in addition to national holidays.

National Association of Child Care Resource & Referral Agencies (NACCRRA)
703-341-4100 | www.naccrra.org

NACCRRA works with more than eight hundred state and local child care resource and referral agencies nationwide. They lead projects that increase the quality and availability of child care professionals, undertake research, and advocate child care policies that positively impact the lives of children and families.

National Association for the Education of Young Children (NAEYC)
800-424-2460 | www.naeyc.org

Founded in 1926, NAEYC has nearly ninety thousand members world-wide. Their mission is to serve and act on behalf of the needs, rights, and well-being of all young children, with primary focus on the provision of educational and developmental services and resources. More information can be found on their website, including a database of schools accredited by them.

National Catholic Educational Association
800-711-6232 | www.ncea.org

This site has a directory for Catholic schools.

National Resource Center for Health and Safety in Child Care (NRC)
800-598-5437 | nrc.uchsc.edu

The NRC is funded by the Maternal and Child Health Bureau of the U.S. Department of Health & Human Services. The NRC's primary mission is to promote health and safety in out-of-home child care settings throughout the nation.

The Department of Early Education and Care (EEC)
617-988-6600 | www.eec.state.ma.us

EEC licenses most child care programs. You can see guidelines on their website and license regulations at www.eec.state.ma.us/oo_licensing.aspx. Programs must meet minimum licensing requirements, which include, but are not limited to, the following:

- All providers, household members in a Family Child Care home, and staff in a Center Based program must have a criminal background check.
- All providers and staff must be certified in first aid and CPR.
- Family Child Care providers must complete a three hour orientation and attend an additional fifteen hours of training every three years.
- Teachers and directors for Child Care Centers must have college courses in child development and one to three years of experience working with children.
- Homes and programs are inspected and must be safe, clean, and of sufficient size as well as pass all local building, health, and lead paint inspections.
- Licensed programs can also be accredited. This means that the program has met even higher standards set by a national organization (such as NAEYC).

The Savvy Source
www.thesavvysource.com

This website has a huge database of preschools. Many have ratings and reviews from parents, while others have the bare-bones details (address, phone number, website), but it's a great place to start searching.

Preschool

Preschool is generally (and vaguely) defined as the period when kids have outgrown daycare, but are too young for kindergarten. Depending on the school or program, children as young as two can qualify. For the purposes of this book, I am defining preschool as a place that has a specific curriculum that focuses on preparing children for school and is for kids 2.9 and above.

Since preschool is not universally available for every child in the United States, most of us have to pay for it if we choose to enroll our kids. The city of Boston has a few slots for children three and four years of age, but not enough for all the eligible kids in the city (see chapter 9 for details on K0 and K1).

As with choosing a daycare, there are many factors in choosing a preschool that will vary in importance for every family. Just a few may include how close the preschool is to your home; what the teacher-student ratio is; is it full-day or half-day; and does it have a playground.

And just like college—don't laugh!—there's no guarantee your child will get in if there is space. While some schools are very open about the fact that there is no criteria for acceptance—it's simply first come, first served—others admit that they do have a criteria, though they tend to be very vague about what it is. Often you'll have to interview with the director and teachers, and so might your child. Sometimes your child will need to spend a couple of hours in the preschool to be evaluated. Also, keep in mind that most, if not all, preschools give preference to siblings, so it is a veritable roll of the dice as to how many seats may be available in any given classroom at any given time. Because many of the city's popular preschools have waitlists, you'll want to apply to more than one. The good news is that a waitlist is *not* a rejection—so keep the faith. As so many families come and go from the city each year, there tends to be a fair amount of movement on the list from the acceptance period (in early March) to the beginning of the school year in September. Still, your best bet is to apply in a timely fashion and to talk to other parents on the playground—they may not be able to get you into your dream preschool, but their advice in the process can be invaluable. The selection of preschools here encompasses well-established programs that are open to the general public.

Boston Preschools

Acorn Center for Early Education and Care
38 Ash Street, Boston
617-635-5129 | www.bcnc.net/childcare.php
Ages: 15 months–5 years
Hours: Year-round, Monday–Friday, 7:30AM–5:30PM
Teacher-student ratio: 1:8
Classrooms: 5
Tuition: $195 per week; toddler rate is $290 per week
Application deadline: Rolling

Bilingual (Chinese-English) child care program that accepts children of all backgrounds and cultures. Creative and developmental learning through songs, stories, role-play, and hands-on activities. Licensed by the Massachusetts Department of Early Education and Care and accredited by the NAEYC. Each classroom has two full-time teachers, one English speaking and one Chinese speaking, and all class activities are conducted in both Chinese and English.

Advent School Early Childhood Center

15 Brimmer Street, Back Bay
617-742-0520 | www.adventschool.org
Ages: 4 years
Hours: Monday–Friday, 8:15AM–3:15PM; Friday, 12:30PM dismissal
Teacher-student ratio: 1:7
Classrooms: 1 preschool classroom
Tuition: $17,600 per year (for children attending five days a week)
Application deadline: January

The Advent School Early Childhood Center offers a program inspired by Italy's Reggio Emilia preschools, where children learn to become reflective problem solvers at a young age. In keeping with the philosophy of their elementary program, teachers integrate all areas of the curriculum and encourage in-depth learning experiences.

Arc-En-Ciel Day Care: Montessori Daycare and Preschool Center

61 Rockwood Street, South Brookline/Jamaica Plain
617-522-0640 | arcencieldaycare.com
Ages: 2 months–5 years
Hours: Monday–Friday, 7:30AM–3:30PM
Teacher-student ratio: 1:8
Classrooms: 1
Tuition: $360 per week (for children attending five days a week)
Application deadline: Rolling

Bilingual French program teaches French to youngsters as a second language and is done through games, songs, and visual movements. Children are encouraged to progress at their own pace, according to their individual needs and abilities. A fun and safe playground is designed to challenge and delight each age group. The director, assistant director, and program coordinators have graduated from reputable, accredited

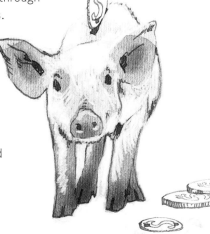

colleges or universities and possess a master's degree in psychology and/or early childhood education.

1 Ashmont Street, Dorchester
617-282-6063 | www.ashmontnurseryschool.com
Ages: 2.9-5 years
Hours: Monday–Friday, 8:30AM–2:45PM
Teacher-student ratio: 4:20 (four adults are three certified teachers and one parent; this is the minimum number of parents and maximum number of students)
Classrooms: 3 spaces (nature, reading, arts and crafts, capped with a playspace)
Tuition: $7,821 per year (for children attending five days a week)
Application deadline: January 15

Ashmont Nursery School is a non-profit, non-sectarian, cooperative preschool. Facilities include a spacious indoor play area with a wide variety of materials and a fully equipped outdoor play yard. The school is licensed by the Massachusetts Department of Early Education and Care (EEC) and accredited by the National Association for the Education of Young Children (NAEYC). The school is a parent-run cooperative, and under the guidance and in partnership with certified teachers, the parents form a community that encourages caring for all of the children and families.

74 Joy Street, Beacon Hill
617-227-0822 | www.bhns.net
Ages: 2-kindergarten
Hours: Half-day; extended hours available
Teacher-student ratio: 1:6
Classrooms: Changes based on enrollment
Tuition: Varies, but for the nursery class for 2.9 and older, five half days is $11,000
Application deadline: January 5

The school leases the entire ground floor and space on the second and third floors at Hill House, a nineteenth century brick building in Beacon Hill. Each classroom is equipped with a book area, a science area, a computer, a water/sand table, a dramatic play area, art supplies, large and small blocks, and a variety of manipulative materials and games. The school library has more than 3,500 books, tapes, and videos. There are two custom-designed, on-site playgrounds, and the school has daily access to a gym for creative movement and dramatic play, special events, and where children can run and play. There is a large, multi-purpose room used for lunch, meetings, and special projects and activities.

☀ Ten Tips from NAEYC

The National Association for the Education of Young Children (NAEYC), founded in 1926, has nearly ninety thousand members worldwide. Here's some advice from them; much more can be found on their website (www.naeyc.org), including a database of schools accredited by them.

1. A good program will provide parents an opportunity to visit, stay a while, and get a good sense of the environment.

2. Parents should ask about and observe group sizes and the number of teaching staff in each classroom. For preschoolers, group size should not exceed twenty children with at least two teaching staff always present.

3. Play, including dramatic play and blocks and active play outdoors, should be integrated into classroom topics of study. Play not only supports children's intellectual development; it is also very important for their physical development.

4. Programs should promote the health and nutrition of children.

5. Children in the program should be engaged with one another and their teachers. Listen and watch for a happy buzz of activity—neither too quiet nor too loud.

6. Teachers should use positive speech and be loving and responsive to a child.

7. A good program should be able to adapt to the needs of each individual child without ignoring the whole group.

8. A high-quality program should have strategies in place to attract and maintain a consistently qualified, well-trained staff and reduce staff turnover.

9. Programs should have a strong connection with the families of each child and the community as well.

10. Check that the program is licensed by the state.

Reprinted with permission by NAEYC

Boston Children's School

8 Whittier Place, Boston
617-367-6239 | www.bostonchildrensschool.org
Ages: 2.9-kindergarten
Hours: Monday–Friday, half day, 8:45AM–1PM; full day, 8:15AM–5:30PM
Teacher-student ratio: 1:8
Classrooms: 6
Tuition: Half day, $12,440 per year; full day, $16,795 per year
Application deadline: January 30

This non-profit school founded in 1965 uses a cognitive developmental approach. Kids from all over the world attend. Supplemental teachers come in to teach, art, music, woodworking, drama, and gymnastics.

Boston Renaissance Charter Public School

250 Stuart Street, Boston
617-357-0900 | www.bostonrenaissance.org
Ages: 4 years and up (Kinder School)
Hours: Monday–Friday, 7:45AM–3:10PM
Teacher-student ratio: 2:20
Classrooms: 11
Tuition: Free
Application deadline: Lottery system; last day of February

The Boston Renaissance Charter Public School is the largest charter school in Boston and has three schools in one facility, the Kinder School, Primary School, and Elementary (which goes to sixth grade). The Kinder School has eleven K1 classrooms for children age four by September 1. Instruction in all subject areas is aligned with the Massachusetts Curriculum Frameworks; the focus is to create strong foundations in the areas of sensory-motor, oral, language, literacy, mathematics, creative arts, and social emotional development.

British School of Boston

416 Pond Street, Jamaica Plain
617-522-2261 | www.britishschool.org/boston
Ages: 3 and toilet trained–13 years
Hours: Monday–Friday, 8:30AM–11:45AM; extended hours available
Teacher-student ratio: 1:16 and 1 assistant
Classrooms: 1 (but changes on enrollment)
Tuition: Half day, $13,100 per year; full day (8:30AM–3:15PM), $24,330 per year
Application deadline: Rolling

The British School of Boston aims to provide a broadly based and tailored British style education for students from nursery age to year 13. BSB's curriculum represents the best of current practice in the United Kingdom, with an international perspective appropriate to its American home.

Commonwealth Children's Center

1 Ashburton Place, Room 105A, Boston
617-727-4802 | www.commchildcenter.com
Ages: 3 months–6 years
Hours: Monday–Friday, 8:15AM–5:30PM
Teacher-student ratio: 1:10
Classrooms: 1
Tuition: Varies depending on child's age and household income
Application deadline: Rolling

A private, non-profit, non-affiliated early childhood educational program that is open to the general public. CCC is governed by a parent-community board. The program is accredited by NAEYC.

Friends Childcare

Brookline: 110 Cypress Street | 617-731-1008
Roslindale: 1195 Centre Street | 617-469-2507
www.friendschildcare.net
Ages: 6 weeks–5 years
Hours: Monday–Friday, 7AM–6PM
Teacher-student ratio: 1:7
Classrooms: 1
Tuition: Varies by hours and days
Application deadline: Rolling

A non-sectarian school that uses a curriculum based on the philosophy of following children's interests. They offer dance, music, yoga, library, computer play, soccer, and summer programs.

Hollow Reed School

93 Sedgwick Street, Jamaica Plain
617-524-4881 | www.hollowreedschool.com
Ages: 2.9–6 years
Hours: Monday–Friday, 8:30AM–5:30PM
Teacher-student ratio: 1:8
Tuition: Varies by hours and day
Application deadline: Rolling

The Hollow Reed School is an independent, family oriented school with an enrollment of fifty students. Curriculum is planned with a view toward fostering the social, emotional, physical, and cognitive growth of the child. There is an emphasis on the arts, learning through play, and a multicultural approach—striving to foster and honor diversity in the curriculum and community.

John Winthrop School

66 Marlborough Street, Boston
617-267-7159 | www.johnwinthropschool.org
Ages: 15 months–5 years
Hours: Monday–Friday, half day, 8:15AM–11:45AM; full day, 8:15AM–3PM; extended day, 8:15AM–5:30PM
Teacher-student ratio: 1:8
Classrooms: 4
Tuition: Varies depending on age and hours; half day, $12,450 per year; extended day, $21,750 per year
Application deadline: Rolling

The school's mission is to foster the social, emotional, and cognitive development of young children. Teachers facilitate the learning process by providing children with opportunities to explore many developmentally appropriate activities and materials, and by allowing them to make decisions in accordance with their own interests.

Kingsley Montessori School

30 Fairfield Street, Boston
617-226-4900 | www.kingsley.org
Ages: 2–6 years
Hours: Monday–Friday, 8:30AM–2:45PM
Teacher-student ratio: 1:8
Classrooms: 6
Tuition: Varies depending on age and hours; half day, $15,500 per year; extended day, $20,100 per year
Application deadline: January 15

Children are encouraged to use their developing knowledge of the world and sense of curiosity to explore. Montessori lessons inculcate basic skills in computation, pre-reading, and pre-writing. In addition to classroom-based learning, preschool students enjoy classes in Spanish, science, art, music, drama, and movement (physical education). Each classroom is multi-aged, and the equipment, materials, and furniture are child-focused and child-sized.

Lee Academy Pilot School

155 Talbot Avenue, Dorchester
617-635-6619 | www.boston.k12.ma.us/leeacademy
Ages: 3–5 years
Hours: Monday–Friday, 9:30AM–3:30PM
Teacher-student ratio: 1:6
Classrooms: 6 plus 1 special needs room
Tuition: Free
Application deadline: Lottery system; January 15

The centerpiece of the Lee Academy's curriculum is an intensive focus on literacy and language development. Employing the latest research and practice-based methods, staff ensure that all children become strong readers and writers.

North End Children's Center

332 Hanover Street, North End
617-643-8007 | www.partners.org/ChildCare/North_End_Center/About.html
Ages: 2.9–7 years
Hours: Monday–Friday, 7:30AM–5:30PM
Teacher-student ratio: 1:10
Classrooms: 3
Tuition: Varies by hours and day
Application deadline: Rolling

Opened over one hundred years ago, the North End Children's Center is one of the country's first child care and early childhood education facilities. It has a child-centered, developmentally based curriculum.

Pine Village Kids

Brighton: 617 Cambridge Street | 617-562-0880
Jamaica Plain: 8 Roanoke Street | 617-522-3716
Newton: 1326 Washington Street | 617-965-2221
Cambridge: 2067 Massachusetts Avenue | 508-212-7486
South End: 700 Harrison Avenue | 617-262-7463
www.pinevillagekids.com
Ages: 2-5 years
Hours: Monday-Friday, half day, 9AM-1PM;
full day, 9AM-4PM; extended day, 8AM-5:30PM
Teacher-student ratio: 2:15
Classrooms: 3
Tuition: Varies depending on hours and days
Application deadline: Rolling

Offers children a Spanish immersion language program naturally infused into a traditional preschool academic curriculum.

South Boston Neighborhood Preschool

1187 Columbia Road, South Boston
617-269-4090 | www.sbnh.org/programs/preschool.html
Ages: 2.9-6 years
Hours: Monday-Friday, 7:30AM-5:30PM
Teacher-student ratio: 1:10
Classrooms: 3
Tuition: $185 per week
Application deadline: Rolling

The South Boston Neighborhood House was founded in 1901 and has a long history of offering programs for children. Its modern child care program is designed primarily for working parents and their children. Agency goals in the provision of quality child care are twofold: providing support to working families and promoting the growth of the children.

Spruce Street Nursery School

5 Avery Place, Boston
617-482-5252 | www.sprucestreetnurseryschool.com
Ages: 2-5 years
Hours: Monday-Friday, 8:30AM-1PM; extended hours available
Teacher-student ratio: 1:4.5
Classrooms: 4
Tuition: Varies depending on hours and days; two mornings,
$6,250 per year; five mornings, $13,500 per year
Application deadline: January 15

Curriculum developed to honor each child's potential at their own pace. Music, art, and children's literature are a large part of the program. The school uses the resources of the city to explore and learn.

Sunrise Learning Academy

131 Cambridge Street, Boston
617-227-6402 | www.sunriselearningacademy.com
Ages: 2.9–5 years
Hours: Monday–Friday, 7AM–6PM
Teacher-student ratio: 1:10
Classrooms: 1
Tuition: Varies depending on days; two days, $110 per week; five days, $280 per week
Application deadline: Rolling

The school's philosophy encourages continuous learning and growth. Through play and active learning, activities help promote each child's social, emotional, physical, and cognitive development. The fundamental philosophy is to provide a safe learning environment, with a trusting and respectful relationship between families and teachers.

United South End Settlements

48 Rutland Street, Boston
617-375-8150 | www.uses.org
Ages: 2 months-5 years
Hours: Monday-Friday, 8AM-6PM
Teacher-Student Ratio: 1:8
Classrooms: 7
Tuition: Varies depending on hours and days; income-eligible financial aid is available
Application deadline: Rolling

United South End Settlements has both an Infant/Toddler and a Preschool program, both accredited by the NAEYC. Their hands-on, developmentally appropriate curriculum addresses the "whole child," so that each child leaves USES socially, emotionally, cognitively, and physically prepared for success in school. The Preschool program serves approximately fifty-two children ages 2.9 through 5 years of age.

The following Boston Ys offer preschool. Slots fill fast and each one has different hours and fees. Call or visit www.ymcaboston.org for details.

Dorchester—Linking Hands Preschool and Toddler Care
102 Columbia Road | 617-445-9622
Ages: 15 months–5 years
Hours: Monday-Friday, 7:30AM–6PM

East Boston—Early Child Care
215 Bremen Street | 617-569-9622
Ages: 15 months–5 years
Hours: Monday-Friday, 7AM–6PM

Roxbury—Preschool at the Branch
285 Martin Luther King Boulevard | 617-427-5300
Ages: 2.9–6 years
Hours: Monday-Friday, 7AM–6PM

West Roxbury—Kids' Stop
1208 VFW Parkway | 617-325-1921
Ages: 2.9–5 years
Hours: Monday-Friday, 7:30AM–6PM

Barely Beyond Boston: Additional Preschool Resources

In the surrounding neighborhoods of Boston, there are dozens, if not hundreds, of excellent preschools to choose from, both public and private. Here are some great resources to help you find the perfect match.

Brookline Early Education Program—Parent Teacher Organization (BEEP PTO)

617-713-5471 | beeppto.weebly.com
Ages: 2.6–4.11 years

BEEP was established over thirty-five years ago to provide high-quality early education to the young children of Brookline. The program currently enrolls over two hundred and fifty families in nineteen classes in all eight Brookline elementary schools, the Lynch Center, and Brookline High School (the Child Study Center).

Center for Families

617-349-6385 | www.cambridgema.gov; Search: Center for Families
Ages: Up to 6 years

Center for Families is a family support program for young families in Cambridge. The program receives support and oversight from the citywide Cambridge 0–8 Council composed of parents, caregivers, and service providers. It is a part of the Department of Human Services Child Care and Family Support Services Division.

In Cambridge, preschool programs at the M. L. King, King Open, East Cambridge, Morse, and Peabody schools are year-round, five-day, full-time programs. The Haggerty Preschool Program is a ten month school-year, half-day program with slots available two or three days a week. Enrollment is ongoing for all preschool programs. Preschool programs serve children 2.9 to 5 years.

Child Care Resource Center
617-547-1063 | www.ccrcinc.org

CCRC promotes the healthy development and well-being of young children in Cambridge, Somerville, and surrounding communities. They provide access to services and resources for families. On their website, you'll find a preschool directory, tips, and other useful information.

Newton Public Schools Early Childhood Program
617-559-6050 | www.newtonpreschool.com
Ages: 3–5 years

The program offers eight integrated preschool classrooms with an enrollment of fifteen to sixteen children per classroom. Integrated classrooms include children with and without disabilities. Each classroom is taught by a master's level teacher and supported by two to four assistant teachers. The curriculum is developmentally appropriate and based on the Massachusetts Curriculum Frameworks. Additionally, the program is accredited by NAEYC.

WarmLines
617-244-4636 | www.warmlines.org

The non-profit organization offers a *Guide to Newton Preschools* for just $15. The 2008–09 edition of the guide included forty-one half-day programs, for ages 2.9 years to kindergarten, with information about hours, fees, and program philosophy. The guide provides helpful guidelines for visiting and choosing a preschool, including a handy checklist. Call or visit their website for more information.

9 Navigating the Public School Jungle

BELIEVE IT OR not, your adorable baby will one day be old enough to go to school. Luckily, the Boston Public Schools are a viable option for

families in the city. Unfortunately, this fact does not make the application and enrollment process any less confusing. To make matters more complex, if you're considering the public school system for elementary school, you have to start thinking and planning for it when your tot is three years old. (Yup! *Three*!)

In the past, if you were like me, you went to the school closest to your house. Period. Today, there are many more options, and in Boston the public schools can seem a bit overwhelming due to its "zone" system. But have no fear. If you do your research you will find the right school for your child. Rest assured that there are many excellent schools in Boston, from public to parochial to private. But just like college, it's a matter of searching for it, interviewing teachers, and visiting campuses.

In this section I will specifically address the Boston Public Schools (BPS) system. Think of it as your roadmap to the enrollment process. While it may seem like a long time until you'll need or use this information, planning ahead can make navigating the elementary school jungle that much easier. Knowing your options early on can help you make other decisions, such as where and when to send your child to preschool.

In chapter 10, you'll find additional resources, with everything from important BPS phone numbers, parent groups, and websites to information for other educational options, such as home schooling, private, parochial, and Montessori schools.

The ABCs

Boston Public Schools main website: www.bostonpublicschools.org

By law, all children in Massachusetts must attend school beginning in September of the calendar year in which they turn six years old (and they must be at least five before school starts). Children go to a school in their geographic zone. There are three zones: East, West, and North. Please note the city is currently considering reconfiguring them, so some changes may occur.

Parents make a wish list of their top choices of schools in their zone and submit them to the BPS. Most people consider it a lottery, but there is actually a system in place, and there are factors that can weight your choices (see below).

The very best thing you can do for yourself and your child is to do your homework—and you can't start too soon. Whatever you do, don't miss the deadlines! A lot of the selection process is based on dates, and if you're late with your paperwork or you're missing something (an immunization form or proof of residency, for example), you will move down on the list.

As you search for schools, talk to as many people as you can, but remember every family has a different notion of their ideal school. So take the time to visit different schools; talk to teachers and to other parents; don't be afraid to ask to sit in a classroom for half the day or speak to the principal; find out what each school offers; sit in on a parent committee meeting; see what extracurricular events the schools schedule in the year; if an after-school program is important to you, scout out schools that offer it. There are neighborhood groups you can join where you can pool research with other parents and get feedback on school visits and share knowledge. You can visit the BPS Family Resource Center in your neighborhood as well. There are an endless amount of variables that will matter to you. Prioritize them, be realistic, and remember, don't be late with your paperwork!

If you don't receive one of your school choices, or if you don't return an application in time, your child will be assigned to the school closest to your home that has an open seat.

Statistics & the Neighborhood Zones

There are currently one hundred and forty-three schools in the BPS system, which includes sixty elementary schools (K–5) and eighteen elementary/middle schools (K–8).

East Zone: Dorchester, Hyde Park, Mattapan, South Boston

West Zone: Jamaica Plain, Roslindale, Roxbury, West Roxbury

North Zone: Allston-Brighton, Back Bay, Charlestown, Downtown, East Boston, Mission Hill, South End

The Schools: A Primer

There are one hundred and forty-three BPS schools, with some that offer K0, K1, K2 and go up to grade five, grade eight, or grade twelve (explanation below).

There are also pilot schools, charter schools, exam schools (for high schools), and schools that offer advanced placement classes (in grades four, five, and six). Here is a breakdown of the terms you need to become familiar with:

K0, K1: There are a limited number of seats available for children ages three to six years at six Early Learning Centers (ELCs) around the city. K0 is for children age three; K1 is for children age four. There are 2,100 seats for K1. Keep in mind that according to the BPS, it figures to have about 26,000 kids enrolled in grades K–5 in 2009 (see the BPS website for statistics). You can see that getting into a K0 or K1 school might be difficult. A couple of the ELCs also offer K2 (which is regular kindergarten) and first grade.

K2: Kindergarten classes for children age five and above. Most children enter BPS at this stage.

Pilot Schools: Pilot schools are part of the school district but have autonomy over budget, staffing, governance, curriculum/assessment, and the school calendar to provide increased flexibility to organize schools and staffing. They were explicitly created to be innovative and for the most part are hugely popular. Wait lists can be ferocious. Overall, about seven thousand kids attend the eighteen pilot schools in Boston.

Charter Schools: Charter schools aren't part of the BPS. They are run by the state and are independent public schools that operate under five-year charters granted by the Commonwealth's Board of Education. They have the freedom to organize around a core mission, curriculum, theme, or teaching method.

Advanced Work: A few of the BPS schools offer Advanced Work Classes (AWC) for students in grades four, five, and six. This is an accelerated academic curriculum for highly motivated, academically capable students and is by invitation only. Kids are tested in the fall of third, fourth, and fifth grade each year.

Exam Schools: Boston has three "examination schools" for grades seven to twelve that admit students on a competitive basis: Boston Latin Academy, Boston Latin School, and the John D. O'Bryant School of Mathematics and Science. Students are admitted to the exam schools based on results of an entrance test and grade point average.

Feeder School: A middle school that guarantees seats to certain elementary schools (eliminating the need to apply to middle schools).

Specials: Subjects such as art, music, science, and physical education are called "specials" and not every school has the same combination. Ask to see what is offered.

The Enrollment Process

Every winter there is a Showcase of Schools held in a large venue where you can see displays of student work, meet school staff, and pick up information on school registration. School Preview Time is held between November and January. You can meet the principal, teachers, and other parents; tour the building; and visit classrooms.

To register your child (for the following school year), you'll need at least three pre-printed proofs of your current address; up-to-date immunization records; and your child's original birth certificate, passport, or I-94 form if you are registering for kindergarten or first grade. Even though you will have to physically go to a Family Resource Center, you can eliminate some of the paperwork by pre-registering online in December. Registration takes place in late January and early February. All of the dates and deadlines can be found on the BPS website.

The Assignment Process

Assignments are made by a computer that is programmed with a mathematical formula. The computer program tries to assign students to their highest listed choice for which they have the highest priority (explanation below).

You can apply for schools in your zone and schools in other zones if the schools are within your walk zone. Citywide K–8 and middle schools are open to all students.

Sometimes a school doesn't have room for every student who lists it as a choice (be prepared for this). When this happens, the computer assigns students based on choice and priorities.

How Priority Placement Works

The highest priority BPS considers for a new student is sibling priority. If requested, BPS tries to place kids in the same family to the same school.

Next up is walk zone priority. Fifty percent of a given school's seats are saved for residents who live less than a mile from an elementary school. Finally, there is the random number placement. The computer gives each application a random number. Random numbers are used to break ties between students who have the same priorities for the school.

If your child is assigned a K0 or K1 spot and ends up staying for first grade as well, they will be assigned to available second grade seats before students new to the BPS or those applying for transfers from other elementary schools.

Assignments are mailed out in March or you can call your Family Resource Center.

Note: Any student who lives in East Boston is guaranteed a seat somewhere in the neighborhood because of the area's geographic location. This applies to students in all grades and programs, K2 through twelfth grade.

The Wait List

If you don't get your first choice, the computer will either assign your child to one of your other choices or put your child on a wait list (or both). Wait list placement depends on when the student applied, sibling priority, the school choices selected on the application, and random number.

Your child can be placed on up to three wait lists. Here's how it works: say you picked five schools for your wish list and you are assigned to your second choice school. You can opt to stay on the wait list for your first choice school. If you are assigned your third choice, you can stay on the wait lists for your first and second choices. If you get your fourth choice, you can be on the wait lists for your top three picks. You can only be on three wait lists at one time. Your child will stay on the wait lists even once school starts, up to the end of January of that school year. Should a seat open for your child in October, you can transfer if you still want that school.

Wait List Information

You can find out your child's wait list status by calling any Family Resource Center at the end of each application period. In August and September, you can also call the School Hotline, 617-635-9046.

A

Adoption

Adoption Community of New England (ACONE)

508-366-6812 | 800-932-3678 | www.adoptioncommunityofne.org
Provides education, information, advocacy, and support to all those
involved in adoption and foster care.

Massachusetts Adoption Resource Exchange (MARE)

617-542-3678 | 800-882-1176 | www.mareinc.org
Places kids in foster care, including sibling groups and children who
are traditionally harder to place.

Single Parents for Adoption of Children Everywhere (SPACE)

508-429-4260 | 800-93-ADOPT | www.geocities.com/odsspace

Support and information organization for single adoptive parents.

Au Pair

Au Pair in America

800-928-7247 | www.aupairinamerica.com
Around since 1986, this company includes screening, medical and liability insurance, a legal J-1 visa, flight arrangements, four-day orientation including Red Cross child safety training, and one year of support.

Au Pair USA

800-287-2477 | www.aupairusa.org
InterExchange is a non-profit organization dedicated to promoting cultural awareness around the world. One way they do this is through their au pair program.

Cultural Care Au Pair

800-333-6056 | www.culturalcare.com
Their main office is in Cambridge, MA, but they prefer to be contacted on the phone or through their website. They claim to have successfully placed more than 75,000 au pairs in U.S. homes since 1989!

B

Babysitting/Nannies Services

Beacon Hill Nannies

617-630-1577 | www.beaconhillnannies.com
Extensive screening of nannies. All have college degrees. Full-time live-in or live-out placements.

Boston's Best Babysitters

617-268-7148 | www.bbbabysitters.com
Offers short- and long-term babysitting care.

Boston Nanny Centre, Inc.

617-527-0114 | www.bostonnanny.com
Founded in 1988, the center offers live-in, live-out, part time, temporary, and overnight nannies.

Care.com

This Waltham-based online business matches up parents with sitters, nannies, as well as tutors and other special services (such as pet care and housekeeping).

Minute Women Family and Home Care

781-862-3300 | www.minutewomen.net
Minute Women is a family-owned business, founded in 1969. They provide live-out nannies, the occasional babysitter, or postpartum overnight care.

Parents in a Pinch

617-739-5437 | www.parentsinapinch.com
Provides nannies and babysitters to families in Massachusetts.

Sitter City

www.sittercity.com
They offer a four-step screening process, free access to background checks, and babysitter video interviews. The site can help you find not just babysitters, but nannies, mother's helpers, doulas, and au pairs.

Birthday Party Venues

Boston Athletic Center

653 Summer Street, Boston
617-269-4300 | www.bostonathleticclub.com
Choose from gym and swim parties, karaoke, sports wall, and more. For kids ages three to twelve.

Boston Children's Museum

300 Congress Street, Boston
617-426-6500 | www.bostonkids.org
Choose from two different birthday packages for a two-hour birthday party. Both include a private room for up to twenty-five guests. Reservations must be made two months in advance, and parties are held Friday to Sunday.

Creative Arts Parties at the Leventhal-Sidman Jewish Community Center

333 Nahanton Street, Newton
617-558-6416 | www.lsjcc.org

Party themes and projects include pottery, woodworking, jewelry making, mosaics, and Princess Parties. Parties are run by experienced staff in state-of-the-art studios. Refreshments are served in a separate function room following the art activity.

Creative Movement and Arts Center

145 Rosemary Street, Needham
781-449-2707 | centers.brighthorizons.com/cmac
Included in the one-and-a-half hour birthday package are two hosts, all paper goods and table settings, along with pre- and post-party clean up. All activities are held in the colorful, fun, and safe gym. Bring your own food, but they'll help you serve it.

Curious Creatures

106R Main Street, Groveland
978-556-5353 | www.curiouscreatures.org
A one-hour hands-on educational program in home or location of choice. A staff member brings a variety of animals and lots of fun facts about the animals for the program. Each program is tailored to suit needs and age group. Party can be for up to twenty children, travel charges apply.

Exxcel Gymnastics & Climbing

88 Wells Avenue, Newton
617-244-3300 | www.exxcel.net
Parties are scheduled on the weekends. Package includes one hour in the gym, thirty minutes in the party rooms, a gift for the birthday boy/girl, and complimentary invitations.

Full Moon Restaurant

344 Huron Avenue, Cambridge
617-354-6699 | www.fullmoonrestaurant.com
You get the run of the Cambridge restaurant. They offer tea parties for eight or more children from 3:15 PM–4:45 PM any afternoon of the week. Included is cake, ice cream, balloons, and decorations.

Gymboree Birthday Parties

109 Oak Street, Newton
617-244-2988 | www.gymboreeclasses.com
The highlight of the party is an hour of fun activities for the birthday boy/girl and their friends. Choose a cake from Party Favors, special Gymboree goody bags, or even a visit from Gymbo the Clown.

Kids Fun Stop

1580 VFW Parkway, West Roxbury

617-325-0800 | www.kidsfunstop.com

An indoor activity center for children up to six years. Reserve the playground for one- and-a-half hours Friday to Sunday. Table settings are provided, but you need to bring your own food.

New Art Center

61 Washington Park, Newtonville

617-964-3424 | www.newartcenter.org

Choose from several party themes. The party includes one hour of art instruction from a professional artist, all art materials, and two party spaces (one for the art, one for the party). You bring the food and table settings, as well as help with the cleanup afterwards.

Puppet Showplace Theatre

32 Station Street, Brookline

617-731-6400 | www.puppetshowplace.org

The theatre offers several options for birthday parties. The party can travel to the theatre and watch a show as a group. After the last performance, you can reserve the lobby for an after-party. The theatre can also host a private party, which offers the party a private performance and exclusive use of the theatre. The theatre can also suggest a touring performer who can perform at your home or location of choice.

The Kid's Place

33 Highland Avenue, Needham

781-444-2325 | www.kidsplace4fun.com

Choose from one main activity plus extras to entertain the birthday guests. Choices include mining for gems and painting a treasure/jewelry box, painting ceramics, making mosaics, tie-dyeing a T-shirt or pillowcase, painting plaster figures, or edible art. Grab bags, cotton candy, face painting, tattoos, nail painting, and more are available to add to the party fun.

Blogs

Braving the BPS Lottery

bravingthelottery.blogspot.com

A blog by the mom of a three-year-old boy. She documents her thoughts on the Boston Public School system.

Foodie Mommy

www.foodiemommy.blogspot.com
This mom, an eighth grade social studies teacher, lives about twenty minutes west of Boston and has been completely obsessed with food since she was little. Her blog offers a selection of family-friendly trips with great foodie finds, restaurant reviews in Greater Boston, and recipes for those that don't want to serve their little ones chicken nuggets every night.

Massachusetts Mom

www.massachusettsmom.blogspot.com
Journalist and an award-winning television producer Anne-Marie Dorning blogs on a variety of topics, such as food, travel, schools, and anything else that tickles her fancy. She also runs www.newenglandmoms.com, a site where moms from all over the region can share information and showcase the best of New England.

C

Childproofing

Great Beginnings

301-417-9702 | www.greatbeginnings.net
Commercial store with an online shopping service.

Heart & Home Baby Safety Inc.

617-332-0398 | www.homebabysafety.com
They provide a home safety survey, as well as products and installation.

Safe Beginnings

800-780-9949 | www.safebeginningschildproofing.com
Safe Beginnings offers complete home childproofing consultation and installation services, including childproof pool fences.

City Parks/Recreation

Brookline Parks and Open Space Division

617-730-2088 | www.brooklinema.gov/parks/system/name.shtml

Cambridge Community Development

617-349-4600 | www.cambridgema.gov/~CDD/cp/parks/index.html

Massachusetts Department of Conservation and Recreation

617-626-1250 | www.mass.gov/dcr

Newton Recreation Areas and Facilities

617-796-1000 | www.ci.newton.ma.us/parks/areas.htm

City Resources

Cambridge Office for Tourism

617-441-2884 | 800-862-5678 | www.cambridge-usa.org

Greater Boston Convention & Visitors Bureau

617-536-4100 | www.bostonusa.com
Information on everything Boston. Go to the Family Friendly Values section for special deals around town.

D

Doulas/Nurses

Birthing Life Doula Care

508-316-1744 | www.birthinglife.com
Birthing Life provides birth doula care, labor support, and postpartum doula services. They also offer homebirth care and comprehensive birth and breastfeeding education for families.

Dona International

888-788-3662 | www.dona.org
Dona International is the premier doula organization. Their nationwide website provides information for doulas, families, and a service to help find local care.

Doula

www.doula.com
Focuses on providing information about doulas to families. Offers practical advice, such as how much a family should expect to pay.

Newborn Nurses
781-690-6776 | www.newbornnurses.org
A private, home health agency that provides lactation/postpartum services to women and babies. Visits by experienced Newborn Nurses and Newborn Nannies help women to overcome the obstacles of breastfeeding in the privacy and comfort of their own homes.

Diaper Services

Diaper Lab
201A Highland Avenue, Somerville
617-623-2848 | www.diaperlab.com

F

Fathers

CPF—The Fatherhood Coalition
617-723-DADS | www.fatherhoodcoalition.org
A non-profit organization advocating for the institution of fatherhood. CPF holds public events, conferences, protests, and rallies and works with the news media to raise public awareness about the importance of fatherhood.

Dads & Donuts
Lowell General Hospital
295 Varnum Avenue, Lowell
877-544-9355 | www.lowellgeneral.org
Bond with your baby and meet new dads.

Fathers and Families
800-439-4805 | www.fathersandfamilies.org
Seeks to protect the child's right to the love and care of both parents after separation or divorce. Fathers and Families also works on court reform that establishes equal rights and responsibilities for both parents.

National Fatherhood Initiative
301-948-0599 | www.fatherhood.org
A nationwide community, the National Fatherhood Initiative aims to ensure that each child has what they need: the love and support of a responsible father.

New Dad Class
Cambridge Health Alliance
1493 Cambridge Street, Cambridge
617-665-4800 | www.cha.harvard.edu; Search: New Dad Class
Led by a pediatric nurse and lactation consultant, groups discuss newborn care, feeding, bathing, sleeping, and other dad issues.

G

GLBT Resources

COLAGE: Greater Boston Chapter
617-714-5327 | www.colage.org/boston
A national movement of youth and adults with one or more LGBTQ parents.

Family Equality Council
617-502-8700 | www.familyequality.org
Works to ensure equality for LGBT families by building community, changing hearts and minds, and advancing social justice for all families.

Gay Fathers of Greater Boston
617-742-7897 | www.gayfathersboston.org
Network of gay fathers with children living with or apart from them.

Gay, Lesbian, and Straight Education Network (GLSEN) Boston
617-536-9669 | www.glsenboston.org
Strives to assure that each member of every school community is valued and respected regardless of sexual orientation or gender identity/ expression.

GLBT Parenting in Greater Boston
www.groups.yahoo.com/group/parenting-in-greater-boston
www.parenting-in-greater-boston@yahoogroups.com
A free Yahoo group that speaks to the social and emotional needs of GLBT parents. They offer a sense of community, an extended family, and a knowing friend.

Greater Boston PFLAG
781-891-5966 | www.gbpflag.org
A group of parents, families, friends, and lesbian, gay, bisexual, and transgender people who are committed to giving support to each other.

Lesbian/Gay Family and Parenting Services
Fenway Community Health Center
7 Haviland Street, Boston
617-927-6243 | www.fenwayhealth.org
Provides medical alternatives to conception, as well as a supporting
network, education, and advocacy.

You're Not Alone—Straight Spouse Support
Newton-Wellesley Hospital
2014 Washington Street (Route 16), Newton
508-429-0969 | www.newellness.com/ynantro.htm
A support group for those currently married to or those who have been
married to a LGBT spouse.

S

School Resources

Archdiocese of Boston
www.bostoncatholic.org
You'll find a list of the dozens of Boston Catholic schools here, from
preschools through high schools.

Boston Parent Organizing Network (BPON)
617-522-2766 | www.bpon.org
Boston Parent Organizing Network's mission is to organize, develop, and
support parents and families who are marginalized by socioeconomic
status, race, language, disability, and immigration status. BPON aims to
work with and hold accountable the Boston Public Schools to provide
an excellent education for all students.

Boston Public Schools Main Switchboard
617-635-9000 | www.bostonpublicschools.org
Alternative Education: 617-635-8035
Boston School Committee: 617-635-9014
English Language Learners: 617-635-9435
Food and Nutrition Services: 617-635-9144
School Hotline (August and September): 617-635-9046
Special Education: 617-635-8599
Transportation: 617-635-9520

Boston Public Schools/Parent Information Centers
East Zone: 1216 Dorchester Avenue, Dorchester | 617-635-8015
North Zone: 55 Malcolm X Boulevard, Roxbury | 617-635-9010
West Zone: 515 Hyde Park Avenue, Roslindale | 617-635-8040

Boston School Options

www.bostonschooloptions.org
Learn about Boston's public schools, plus the thirty-two suburban school districts accessible via the Metco program. Funding for the website was provided by the Boston Foundation.

Countdown to Kindergarten

617-63-LEARN | www.countdowntokindergarten.org
The collaborative Countdown to Kindergarten organization engages families, educators, and the community in a citywide effort to enhance early learning opportunities and to support the transition into kindergarten. The Mayor of Boston, the Boston School Committee, and the Superintendent of schools partner with twenty-eight local organizations to implement a school readiness campaign.

Homeschooling Together

www.home.comcast.net/~jrsladkey/hst/
An Arlington group with over two hundred families with children from infants to teenagers.

Massachusetts Home Learning Association

www.mhla.org
MHLA maintains a list of support groups containing contact information for homeschooling families.

Montessori Schools of Massachusetts

www.msmresources.org
MSM is a regional membership organization committed to promoting knowledge and understanding of Montessori. You can find a database of schools on their website.

National Association of Independent Schools

202-973-9700 | www.nais.org
A membership organization with 501(c)(3) non-profit status. It represents approximately thirteen hundred independent schools and associations in the United States.

National Catholic Educational Association

800-711-6232 | www.ncea.org
This site will give you the scoop on private, Catholic education from educators and institutions serving students in elementary schools, secondary schools, colleges, and universities.

Pilot School Information

617-421-0134 | www.ccebos.org; Search: Pilot Schools
The Center for Collaborative Education, a non-profit education organization, provides the pilot schools with coordination support and assistance, including coaching services, professional development, advocacy, and research and evaluation.

The Savvy Source

www.thesavvysource.com
Preschool ratings and reviews for schools around the country.

West Zone Parents Group

www.groups.yahoo.com/group/westzoneparents
The West Zone Parents Group (WZPG) is a volunteer-run group of parents who are considering enrolling their children in the Boston Public Schools (BPS). Members meet to share information and help one another understand the process of choosing and registering for a school in Boston.

Single Parents

I Heart Single Parents

www.iheartsingleparents.com
An online nationwide community for single parents.

SingleDad.com

www.singledad.com
An online, nationwide network of divorced, widowed, and remarried single dads.

Single Mothers by Choice

617-964-9949 | www.singlemothersbychoice.com
A group that aims to provide support and information to single women who are considering, or who have chosen, single motherhood.

Single Parents Boston

www.singleparentsboston.com
One-on-one matchmaking site.

Special Needs

Federation for Children with Special Needs
617-236-7210 | 800-331-0688 | http://fcsn.org
A center for parents and parent organizations to work together for children with special needs.

Urban PRIDE
617-989-3929 | www.urbanpride.org
Founded to empower parents of children with special needs.

W

Websites

Boston and Massachusetts Events Calendar
www.cityofboston.gov/calendar/

Boston Central
www.bostoncentral.com
An online center for Boston families with calendars and listings.

Boston Mamas
bostonmamas.com
Boston Mamas was developed, designed, and founded by Christine Koh, a Boston mama with a passion for people, communication, art, food, retail, web surfing, and all things mama-related.

Boston.com Moms
www.boston.com/moms
The Boston Globe's section of mom-related content.

Boston-Online
www.boston-online.com
Very useful site with links to all sorts of Boston stuff, including where to find public bathrooms and Boston etiquette. It's a humorous but accurate site that doesn't take itself too seriously.

Boston Parents Paper
617-522-1515 | www.bostonparentspaper.com
A leading online stop for parents that complements the print publication.

Boston Parents Wiki
www.bostonparentswiki.com

A free online resource for parents about services, stores, and things to do for kids in the city. Parents can offer reviews about their own Beantown experiences.

Brand New Dad

www.brandnewdad.com
Social network and resource center for new dads and expectant fathers.

DailyCandy Boston Kids

www.dailycandy.com/kids/boston
Disclosure: I write this. It's a fun resource for parents, featuring everything from new products to day trips to services.

GardenMoms

gardenmoms.findsmithgroups.com
A member group which is an important resource and support network for countless parents, both new and experienced.

GoCityKids

www.gocitykids.com
Find the lowdown on everything to do around Boston with children, includes a daily calendar of happenings around town.

LilaGuide

www.lilaguide.com/city-boston-ma
Another source for events, discussion boards, groups, and reviews.

Mom's & Dad's Guide

www.momsanddadsguide.com
An online guide filled with activities and events to entertain the family year-round. The guide is divided into the South Shore, MetroSouth, and MetroWest.

New England Mom

www.newenglandmoms.com
A site where moms from all over the region can share information and showcase the best of New England.

Parent Zone

www.family.go.com; Search: Boston
Find family-friendly events and a directory of parent resources.

Calendar of Events

Just some of Boston's annual events that families won't want to miss.

January

Japanese New Year

617-426-6500 | www.bostonkids.org
Celebrate at the Children's Museum: arts and crafts, demonstrations, music, and more.

March

St. Patrick's Day Parade/ Evacuation Day

www.saintpatricksdayparade.com/boston
Head to South Boston for this annual parade where Boston's Irish-American families (and of course Bostonians from every other background!) show their ancestral pride.

April

Boston Marathon

617-236-1652 | www.bostonmarathon.com
The oldest marathon in the U.S. Grab the kids and watch on the sidelines, anywhere along the twenty-six miles from Hopkinton to Wellesley to Newton to Brookline to the finish line in Copley Square.

Swan Boats Return to Public Garden

617-522-1966 | www.swanboats.com
Perfect for families with little ones, float around the Public Garden's pond in a giant swan—and visit Mrs. Mallard and the ducklings while you're there.

May

Lilac Sunday

617-524-1718 | www.arboretum.harvard.edu
Have your kids take you to admire the two hundred and fifty different blooms at Arnold Arboretum on Mother's Day—and of course enjoy some family time while you're there.

Make Way for Ducklings Parade (Mother's Day)

617-723-8144 | www.friendsofthepublicgarden.org/kids
Register at noon at Boston Common to have your own dressed up tot march with the other ducklings.

Wake Up the Earth Festival

617-524-6373 | www.spontaneouscelebrations.org
Jamaica Plain's annual festival celebrates what can be accomplished when the entire community comes together.

June

Art in the Park Festival (DeCordova Museum)

781-259-8355 | www.decordova.org
Activities for children; music; entertainment—a great time to check out all that the sculpture park and museum have to offer.

Dragon Boat Festival

www.bostondragonboat.org
Watch the beautiful boats race along the Charles River celebrating the 2,300-year-old tradition of dragon boating—stick around for the Chinese dance, music, food, and other fun activities.

Free Friday Flicks at the Hatch Shell

617-787-7200 | www.wbz.com
Summer program sponsored by WBZ, usually features family fare—bring blankets in case the little ones fade early.

Jimmy Fund Scooper Bowl

800-52-JIMMY | www.jimmyfund.org
Delicious ice cream fundraiser in the middle of Boston's City Hall Plaza.

July

Boston Harborfest

617-227-1528 | www.bostonharborfest.com
Boston celebrates the waterfront with events
through the week of Independence Day.

Boston Pops Fourth of July Concert

www.july4th.org
Pack a picnic, some games, and spend the
Fourth of July in front of the Hatch Shell.

North End Italian Festivals

www.stanthonysfeast.com
Celebrating saints with Italian feasts and
parades over several weekends.

August

August Moon Festival

Join the moon-watching parties and kids can
bring/make their own lanterns at Chinatown's
annual festival. Enjoy the parade, music, and
food.

September

The Big E

413-737-2443 | www.thebige.com
The Eastern States Exposition in Springfield
has agricultural events, amusement rides,
music, parades, and more.

October

Jamaica Pond Lantern Festival

617-524-6373 | www.spontaneouscelebra-
tions.org
Thousands flock to this event to walk around
the pond with lanterns. Kids often come in
costume.

November

Boston Common Frog Pond

617-635-2120 | www.bostoncommonfrog-
pond.org
Time to embrace the winter season as the
pond opens up for ice-skating.

Holiday Lighting Ceremony

617-523-1300 | www.faneuilhallmarketplace.
com
Kick off the holiday season at Faneuil Hall's
Lighting Ceremony. Performances and food all
day will get you and the little ones in the spirit.

December

Christmas Revels

617-972-8300 | www.revels.org
Winter Solstice celebration at Harvard's Sand-
ers Theatre. Every year features a different
theme, and there's plenty of interaction with
the audience—lots of singing! A great holiday
tradition and a real hit with the kids.

First Night

617-542-1399 | www.firstnight.org
New Year's Eve celebration for everyone,
with more than two hundred and fifty events
throughout the city. Buy a button to gain admission to all the festivities in dozens of venues.

Tree Lightings

The two biggies are the *Prudential Holiday
Tree Lighting* and the *Boston Common Holiday
Lighting* the first weekend of this month.

Acknowledgments

No matter whose name graces the cover of a book, it is never a one-person operation. I have many people to thank for their support, information, guidance, and love.

Publisher Nicole Vecchiotti deserves an award for her patience with me, when deadlines sailed on by and as the book changed focus time and time again. Her particular care and editorial guidance cannot be matched. The Union Park Press staff, Erin Whinnery, James Duggan, Corey Major, and in particular, Jossie Auerbach, were invaluable to me.

I owe a debt of gratitude to Dr. Richard Ferber, *Boston Parents Paper* magazine editor Deirdre Wilson, Isis Maternity founder Johanna McChesney, and *Boston Globe* columnist Robin Abrahams (Miss Conduct), who so generously contributed to the book with their wisdom.

So many organizations opened their doors to me—too many to list—but my sincere thanks to everyone who was so helpful and excited to be a part of this project.

My friends served as readers, critics, resources, and researchers. Thanks to all of you, but especially Elizabeth, Katie, Hilary, and Lisa. You know I couldn't do much without your help and encouragement.

Finally, I must sincerely thank my husband Rob, whose support never wavers, and of course, my daughter Sadie, without whom I never would have written this book.

About the...

Publisher

Started by **NICOLE VECCHIOTTI** in 2007, Union Park Press is a local, independent publisher specializing in books about the arts, history, and culture of Boston and New England. This book is dedicated to Nicole's two Boston babies: Amelia and Ethan, and to all our friends big and little from the parks, playgroups, and preschool—who added wisdom and insight every step of the way. Read local! www.unionparkpress.com

Writer

KIM FOLEY MACKINNON is the editor of *DailyCandy Boston Kids* as well as a travel writer and journalist. Her articles have appeared in *The Boston Globe, Global Traveler, Business Traveler, Boston Herald,* and *Parents,* among others. She is the author of numerous guidebooks, including *Boston for Families.* www.kfmwriter.com

Illustrator

KAREN KLASSEN is an award-winning freelance illustrator and mixed media artist. Communicating through imagery is what drew her to the illustration program at Alberta College of Art & Design, and since graduation, has enjoyed creating meaningful images for a wide variety of clients. A few of the areas she's worked in include: advertising, editorial, annual reports, fashion, and publishing. She is inspired by all things vintage—paper, textiles, patterns and colors, has really nice clients, and loves to make images. www.karenklassen.com

Book Designer

ELIZABETH LAWRENCE is an award-winning freelance graphic designer who often explains what book design is. She has enjoyed designing books and other information systems for ten years, and she teaches various design courses at Massachusetts universities. www.elizabethl.com

Notes

Notes